Praise for *Breathe Into Wisdom* and Susan's work

"Rothfuss delivers on her intention to enlighten her readers as she invites them 'to imagine you and I are sitting pleasantly in conversation.' I immediately relaxed and settled into the conversation with her, answering her tales in my own mind as my story followed along with hers. I did not want to stop our journey once begun."

Barbara Parton – Owner Advocate Conversations

Brimming with wisdom gained through experience, *Breathe Into Wisdom* offers clear and grounded steps to personal transformation. Susan Rothfuss has given us a road map of transformational truths, that when practiced, awaken the gift of wisdom that lies within each of us.

Sharon King O'Connor – Licensed Professional Counselor, Professional Educator, Consultant and Licensed in Integrative Medicine

"An intriguing read filled with inspiration."

Clay Dobrovolec

Susan Rothfuss aptly leads and teaches us how to *BREATHE INTO WISDOM*. Her skills as a speaker and motivator shine through as she tells us her story. She offers simple, thoughtful, and constructive tasks as she helps us weave our way to our own Wisdom. I completed the book finding that I'd already effectively spoken to my ego and am on the lookout for my own simple symbolic "black dot."

I found breathing into wisdom, to be very beneficial, informative, exciting and enlightening. I look forward to furthering my exploration following *Breathe Into Wisdom's* recommendations.

Joann Williams

"I've made more progress toward my own goals in my first three sessions with Susan than in two years with a therapist."

Danielle Frazer

Susan has an incredible knack of being able to rise above her personal experiences to see how they can enrich not just her own life, but every other person's life. Her life story validates mine and yours.

Julie Sigler

Breathe
INTO
WISDOM

IT'S THERE...
IT'S YOURS...
USE IT!

BREATHE INTO WISDOM
It's There ... It's Yours ... Use It!

Published by:
Transformation Books
211 Pauline Drive #513
York, PA 17402
www.TransformationBooks.com

ISBN: 978-0-9968271-1-9
Library of Congress Control Number: 2015958516

Book Midwife: Carrie Jareed
Cover Design by: Thomas Phillips
Layout and typesetting by: Ranilo Cabo
Editor: Allison Saia
Proofreader: Michelle Cohen
Photos by: Scott Rosenfeld Photography, ScottRosenfeldPhoto.com

Printed in the United States of America

Table of Contents

Special Thanks

This book had several angels who helped make its publication possible. Your generosity of spirit allowed this book to reach my readers' hands and hearts.
Thank you!

Kathleen Bibbins
Judy Cotter
Tom and Wilma Kehler
Tim and Laura Kowalski
Frank and Sally Lopez
Beth Manning
Maria Manning- Floch
Penny Manning
Barbara Parton
Jane and Greg Reid
Kate Sanford
Jim Wild

Deep gratitude goes to those who were early readers:
Penny Manning, Michael LeFevre and Melany Mack

This book is dedicated to:

My grandmother, Georgia Crowl,
who loved me simply because I was.
My parents, John and Kathryn Rothfuss,
who were my biggest fans.
My business partner and friend Penny Manning who made
me believe this book was possible.

And most especially
My wise and loving Michael, who allows me to be who I am
and supports me on my path to becoming. I love you!

Beginning

As we begin this journey together, I encourage you to imagine you and I are sitting pleasantly in conversation. This is my most comfortable mindset; and I invite you to join me. My life experiences and your life experiences are about to meet. We will be learning about one another, sometimes in serious conversation, sometimes laughing and playful. To get the most out of this experience, may I suggest you sit back, relax and open your mind to possibility?

This is a book about personal transformation. If this is your introduction to personal transformation, rest assured any transformation you experience will be because it is what your spirit yearns to do. The lessons contained in this book will never replace the experiences you will live through. The suggestions and lessons provided may help you breathe through your own life experiences and crises into your highest and best life.

We humans have a wide array of ongoing inputs creating the "who" of who we are. Our family of origin, our communities, our caretakers, our educational systems, our occupations all mold and shape who we are. But what if you could be responsible for shaping or reshaping the essence of who you are? What would you change? How would you change? Who would you like to become? What would your highest and best self be? That is what this book is about. It is a simple guide to lead you into your own transformation.

Some of the ideas presented may be familiar to you, while others may be new. At first you may think, "I don't need to know this. I already have a comfortable mindset where this subject is concerned." But like friends getting to know one another, you continue to listen or read and feel a little poke in your psyche. Pay attention, that poke may be "pay dirt" for you. It may be the tiny seed that needs a place to germinate and grow into a helpful change of mind. You are then invited to change your perspective to get a different view of something you have seen before.

Why would I suggest this? Because it is what I have experienced time after time.. When we dig into a new idea, it may be uncomfortable at first. Digging into it, we resist, we discard, we test, we learn. Often the learning turns into growth. Sometimes the learning teaches us to cautiously avoid. In either case, we have learned something new. That new learning transforms us in some way large or small.

One of the transformative experiences in my life happened when some of the newer members of the non-profit Board of Directors of a local Chamber of Commerce questioned the Letter of Agreement between my company and the Chamber. The Letter of Agreement had been in place for 16 years and adjusted every one or two years and re-signed when changes were made. I was totally blindsided. That would have been the perfect time for me to breathe very deeply and to remember to do so every day during each challenge I would meet over the next two years. I didn't know then how to breathe into wisdom. I didn't even know it was possible. What I learned over the next six years provided me with life affirming answers. Sometimes our crises are our greatest teachers, if we are willing to learn from them. This crisis offered me even greater lessons than any formal education I have experienced.

So how might you use this book? It is entirely up to you! People learn in very different ways. Some are sequential learners and like to read from beginning to end. Others might use it as a survey book – simply read the chapters that interest you and return when you have another question that a chapter title seems to address. Finally, I encourage you to keep the book handy and use the book as a resource. You will find a resource list in the appendix at the back of the book with websites and book titles developed and written by wise women and men, who are leaders in their fields, as well as spiritual entrepreneurs and transformational authors, speakers and teachers whom I reference throughout this book.

Occasionally you will see this icon represents the *Breathe Into Wisdom Workbook*. This workbook is a tool for your use to record your thoughts and experiences as you reflect on what you learn in each chapter. If you would like to purchase the companion workbook, go to *www.skrcoaching.com* and click on the Beathe Into Wisdom tab. Once there you will see the workbook symbol. The entire workbook is in a fillable PDF format. You can also print the entire workbook out and fill it in by hand, if you wish.

On this journey we call life, we all begin by learning to "Breathe." We stop learning when we stop breathing. So join me in a deep, cleansing breath. Let's begin. You may choose to close your eyes and bow your head. When we close our eyes the brain quiets down and when we bow our head the body quiets down. A cleansing breath is achieved by deeply breathing in through the nose and slowly out through the mouth. Be sure to breathe deeply enough to fill your belly, and the lower lobes of your lungs. You will feel your ribs expand. Hold the breath for a few seconds and then very slowly breathe out deeply through your mouth with an "ahhh" sound. Repeat several times. Be in no hurry. This is a signal to your brain and the essence of who you are that you are ready to connect.

Part One

Breathe

Chapter 1

Making Change

With each breath, we change. Cells slough off, thoughts are created, and we move on. Our actions create something new and different. The recently used dishtowel is no longer dry. Change happens. It is inevitable. Change. The Miriam Webster definition of "change," as an intransitive verb, is "to undergo transformation," as in "winter changed to spring." I like that, because transformation is really what this book is about. So I will be using the words "change" and "transformation" interchangeably.

Change is really uncomfortable for many people. Change is so frightening that we are willing to put up with a lot before we entertain the notion of taking on change. It's not unusual to hear, "I want to change but I don't even know where to begin." You may have said it or heard it over and over. It might be said with resignation, "I am just not happy in my job" or marriage or ... well, you name it. It might be shouted with even more vigor, "I am done. I'm not taking this anymore!" You can bet whatever triggered the outburst has occurred before and a change is desired. The problem is, what comes next? Where does change begin?

Ask yourself, what now? How do I even begin to change this situation? Many years ago, I attended a Women's Automotive Group meeting. Several of us were in difficult situations at work. Someone said, "I'd really like to make a change but..." and one of our members volunteered to lead a session on change. This was in the 1980s and women were generally struggling to establish a presence in management within the automotive industry. The topic of change resonated with our membership. We were rapt with attention and most of us eagerly took notes.

The advice we received was quite simple. There are three things you need for change to take place:

1. *You have to be uncomfortable enough in your current situation to be willing to tackle the fear and work to create the change you hope to achieve.*
2. *You know what outcome you want once the change has taken place.*
3. *You don't need to know the whole process. You only need to know the first step toward the change you want.*

Really? Really! This is so true that I am surprised it is not taught in schools to every student. It is a blueprint for creating the life you want, one step at a time.

How Does Change Begin?

Not long after my first husband left me, I knew I needed to change my career. I loved my job, but the facts were in front of me. I could not support my child and myself with any quality of life on the salary I was earning at a non-profit youth service organization. I began to think about going to graduate school. Women were just beginning to be welcomed into law schools, business schools and medical schools. I had successfully managed fundraising programs in my current position and I was good at managing money. I was comfortable with public speaking and group facilitation. What to do?

The idea was just a tiny seed, but it was there. A few weeks later, I was standing in line at a church potluck when Larry, who I did not know well, engaged me in conversation. I mentioned I was thinking about going back to school. We lived in a university community so it was not surprising that he was employed at the university. He asked what I was thinking about and I replied, "Maybe get my M.B.A." His comment, "You'd be great!" was the fertilizer that my little "change" seed needed. It turned out Larry was on the faculty of the College of Business at Michigan State University in the external world, but he and his wife were "angels" in my life.

At this point I had no idea what lay ahead, but I was practicing Step 3. You don't need to know the whole process. You only need to know the first step toward the change you want. I wanted a Master of Business Administration degree. To begin the process I needed to score high enough on the GMAT, an examination required for entry into the Graduate School of Business at Michigan State University's MBA program. Math was my weak point. I decided to go back to Algebra 1 and work my way through Statistics to prepare for that GMAT.

I registered at a local community college to take the math classes that were sadly lacking in my undergraduate program. I took one class every term for four terms. Over the next twelve months, I refreshed my high school Algebra, and completed Algebra II, Trig and an introduction to Statistics. At the same time I prepared for and passed the GMAT. I applied to the university and was accepted. I was planning to continue working full-time at my current position and taking one class a term at the university. As a single mom, full-time employee and part-time student, my plate was full!

About the time I completed my second term in the MBA program, my daughter and I were attending our church family camp and I was walking up a hill (which turned out to be an apt metaphor) when Larry, who was now my advisor in graduate school, said, "You need to be in school full-time." That was just impossible and I told him I couldn't afford to quit my job. I had a mortgage and car payment, insurance, utilities, life's expenses to cover and a child to raise. He said, "You can get a Grad Assistant position and I know just the one."

But the Graduate Assistantship wasn't going to cover the additional expenses of full-time tuition and books. When I expressed my concern to my now professor and mentor, he told me to check with the Dean's office. They might have some assistance available. I met with the Dean of the Business school and was told there might be a special stipend for a single mother returning to school. Remember, this was the 1980s and women were just beginning to return for MBA and law degrees. The next day I received a call confirming I would receive $500 per term! It was truly manna from heaven. My needs were being met. Now, 30 years later, it dawns on me that just maybe that manna came from a certain professor and his wife – but I have never known for sure. I just know it was the difference between being able to go to school full-time at that point in my life or not.

The next thing I knew, I was resigning from my full-time position after being hired as a Grad Assistant in the Executive MBA program at Michigan State University. It was an ideal position for a student, but it paid less than half of my previous salary! That was challenging enough for a single mom, but I was required to work one night a week every week classes were in session. I had a daughter who needed child care in the evening and how could I pay for that? How would I find anyone reliable enough to care for her, come rain or shine?

Enter another angel, Katie. I had met Katie years before, at my first professional job. We were fast friends and she had raised four beautiful daughters. She offered to be there for me for the next two years; expecting no pay, taking care of Amy each week until I returned home from work about midnight. The angels in my life were unexpected and extraordinary in their generosity. When I needed them, they appeared. I was taking the steps, one at a time, to achieve the change I wanted. Two years later, after completing a marathon of steps, I had my M.B.A!

Following the Steps to Create Change

Let's look at that again. I was thrown into a position I never expected and didn't want – divorced and a single mother. I had no idea what lay ahead. I knew things needed to change. (Remember, this is Step 1.) I couldn't survive on what I was making. My situation was too uncomfortable for me to remain stagnant.

I needed to make more money. But how could I? (This is Step 2.) I decided to go to graduate school and earn a Master of Business Administration.

Where would I begin? What was the next step to take on my path of change? Professor Larry facilitated Step 3 for me. I had no idea what it would take. I had no way of knowing I was embarking on the most difficult educational challenge of my life. If I had known all of this, I might have decided to "stay put." But I took that first step. I registered for that first math class, something I never expected or wanted to do, but I knew that was a place of academic weakness for me. My journey had begun.

Change is a path that rolls out before you even initiate the first step. It won't be easy and it may not be straight. You may be climbing your way up a rocky mountain, but you will know where to take the next step. That's the thing about change. You don't have to know all the steps before you start. You simply need to take that first step.

Transformation begins with a change. Sometimes change comes in small, baby steps. Sometimes it comes rushing through our lives like a tsunami. Either way you will not be the same person once the process begins. And you certainly aren't the same when the process concludes. Through it all, the important thing to remember is ... breathe.

Creating Change in Your Life

Do you have something you want to change in your life? Is it frightening to think about? Can you imagine what your life would be like if you made that change? Are you ready yet or will it take more time? Will waiting change anything? It's possible. But unless you expect some external factor to change your life so significantly that you won't need to initiate the change yourself, you might want to think about beginning the transformation for yourself right now.

My journey took almost four years from start to finish. It was frightening and difficult and I had a number of misgivings during that time. But through it all, I never doubted it was possible. Not that I was a great student, or that the financial challenges weren't worrisome. But I knew if I could break each challenge down into small enough bits, I could succeed. I did, and so can you.

How do you build an Empire State Building? One brick at a time. That was the one piece of information that was missing from the session on Change back in the 1980s. That is Step 4. It is okay to take as much time as you need or move as quickly as you like. If you are a sprinter – go for it. If you prefer to move at a slower pace, that is fine too. The important thing to understand about transformation is that we can plan, but sometimes we are just not the one in the driver's seat.

The tsunami that took over my life when my husband wanted a divorce created an opportunity for transformation. Not that I wanted any transformation right then, but I got it. The first change was suddenly becoming a single parent. With that hand being dealt, I took it from there. I thought about going to graduate school. That was the tiny seed. That transformational seed took root in the form of Professor Larry saying, "You'd be great." Once those words were spoken, the path was laid out before me. I didn't know it at the time but, for me, there was no turning back. Did my M.B.A. make me who I am today?

No. But the experience of tackling something about which I knew nothing, working hard at it for years and successfully reaching my goal, did. Those are some of the things that made me the person I am today and continue to encourage me to "continue to become." My tiny change seed germinated into an all-encompassing life change one day at a time.

What can you imagine changing in your life? What change would you make to create your highest and best life? What does a day in your life lived with joy and exuberance look like? How does it feel? Where would you be? With whom would you share it? Take some time to answer these questions before you move on to the next chapter. Relax and remember to take a deep belly breath to get in touch with your essence before you answer those questions. Don't worry. No one will grade your answers. In fact, your answers may change a dozen or more times as you continue reading and living. There may be many alterations again as you begin to follow your path. That is all part of the process – and it is a process. It is not the completion of the process, but going through the process where the learning takes place.

Breathe

I breathe in, I breathe out, I have changed.
With each breath my body transforms.
I breathe deeply, focusing, delving into the wisdom within.
I breathe out.

I breathe into the question for which I am seeking an answer.

I breathe in deeply, slowly, deliciously.
I breathe out deeply, slowly with relief.

I breathe in,
Into the wisdom where I search for the answer.
As I breathe out slowly the answer presents itself.

I breathe in. I breathe out.
My understanding has changed.
Wisdom transforms my understanding.

My body is transformed.
My mind is transformed.
My spirit is transformed.
The world is transformed.

Breathe in. Breathe out.
Breathe!

Breathe

Chapter 2

Attitude is Everything

Attitude is everything, or at least affects everything we do. The only thing over which you really have control in your life is your attitude. That's right, you can control your attitude. You can't fully control your health. You can concentrate on eating a healthy diet and getting appropriate exercise. You can tend to your medical needs and even choose a healthy environment. I know a man who did all of those things and died way too young from liver cancer. He controlled what he thought would help him live a long life. He was unable to control how long he would live.

You can study hard and get a good education that leads to a good job. You can work to improve your skills and get promoted. When the next economic downturn happens, you may find yourself unemployed. Your financial picture can change in an instant.

You can choose to marry or not. You may choose the most wonderful partner. You may even be able to choose if and when to add to your family. But you actually have little or no control over what will happen to you or others in your life. When challenging things happen, the only thing you can control is your attitude. Good things happen, bad things happen, unexpected things happen, expected things happen, and then shocking things happen. Through it all, your attitude is one thing you can count on controlling.

You are the only Person You Can Change

One of the most important things to remember on your life's journey is that you cannot change anyone else. The only person you can change is yourself. I believe it's best to begin with your attitude. When illness strikes, unemployment knocks on your door, love subsides, or challenges arise, your attitude will strongly affect how you deal with each experience.

For a few years, I taught automotive dealership personnel how to deal with customers in a way that would likely "satisfy" them when they came into dealerships with problems. Attitude was the first thing we talked about, because it is so crucial to successful communication with others and with yourself. You have no idea what has happened to every person who has or will cross your path. Their attitudes are influenced by what has happened to them just as yours are influenced by what happens to you. Often you can't control what happens in your daily life. You can try and sometimes you will succeed. What you can control is your attitude toward what happens in your life. If you were always successful in that, you probably wouldn't have picked up this book. If I could have controlled everything in my life I wouldn't have written this book, because I wouldn't have anything to share with you on the subject.

Many things have happened that I couldn't control. Sometimes it turned out to be a good thing, although I wouldn't have said that at the time. The stories I share are true-life stories; and I share them to illustrate how the strategies I live by work for me when I apply them.

Breathe
Sometimes it takes a long time to remember to breathe. Sometimes I forget to forgive, or ask questions, or share information, or remember that I am really a spirit having a human experience. When I remember to apply what I have learned, my life lights up and joy surrounds me. Good things happen easily. What I yearn for presents itself without my effort. Life is good. That hasn't always been true for me. I understand at any moment, it could change.

I've lived a far from perfect life. I have been hurt, sad, sick and divorced. I have been blackballed, experienced sexual harassment, played the victim in a few relationships and worked in psychologically toxic situations for years at a time. I do know a thing or two about life's disappointments. But through each one, I kept breathing. I didn't know at the time how important that was. I didn't realize how close I was to reaching a Wisdom that could help me then, but I did maintain a hopeful attitude.

The Attitude of Hope

Several years into the economic downturn of the early 2000s, I was in a business meeting discussing possible ways to improve membership numbers in our client's non-profit organization. I said we hoped the economy would begin to recover based on the Oakland County Economic Report prepared by two University of Michigan economists. A very cynical young woman, who sat on the Board of Directors, decried my comment that I "hoped" something would occur. "Hope is not a strategy!" she said.

Hope may not be taught in any M.B.A. class, but it should be. She believed hope doesn't make anything happen. She was right, in a way. Hope is an attitude. I believe in hope. It has served me well throughout my life in both the short term and long term. I see hope as a promise to myself: a promise that I will look for progress. I will focus on the good, the joy, the unmistakable signs of happiness, contentment and love in life. That stirring of possibility, where none has been seen for some time, can be attributed to hope. Hope alone will not accomplish anything. Hope combined with responsible actions does help us put one foot in front of the other as we move into what we <u>hope</u> will be a better situation, a better outcome, a better end, a change.

In my opinion, the attitude of hope is often the seed that allows us to take that first step in the change process: be uncomfortable enough in your current situation that you are willing to tackle the fear and work to create the change you hope to achieve. By having hope, you are focusing on a more positive outcome. That focus can make the difference in our lives on a daily basis. In other words, our expectation that something better will occur increases the odds that is just what will happen. More on that when we learn about Creating Your Own Reality in Chapter 11.

Simple Shifts

There are other ways you can change your life by changing your attitude with small, simple shifts in how you understand everyday things. Twenty or more years ago, I began to walk each morning with my neighbor. I didn't know her well, but I wanted to have a reason to strike up a conversation with her. I asked if she would consider walking a few mornings a week with me. She agreed and it was the beginning of a lovely friendship. We would walk and talk. I know we both did it on days we didn't feel like it, just because we wanted to have a chance to catch up with each other. We walked almost every day. Our attitudes had changed – we weren't walking simply to exercise our bodies; we were walking to connect our souls.

A few years later, my husband and I enlarged the gardening area of our back yard. In fact we tripled the area where I could plant flowers. I was so excited about the beautiful possibilities I could create. What I hadn't factored in was the weeding that accompanied the enlarged area. I hated pulling weeds. It was such a chore. I loved planting, and even preparing the beds. I didn't mind cleaning up the garden in the fall and preparing it for the winter. What I really enjoyed was walking around the garden and admiring new buds, watching their progression to full bloom. It gave me pride in knowing I had worked hard to design, plan and plant it.

In fact, each morning after my walk with our neighbor, I would go into the backyard to cool down. As I walked and looked, I would bend down and pluck out a weed here and there. One morning, I really got into it and an idea came to me. If I loved being in the garden among the flowers and plants why couldn't I think of pulling those weeds as part of my hobby too? Instead of thinking of it as a chore, I began to think of it as an opportunity to spend more time in one of my favorite places. From that day on, I have never minded pulling a weed. My daughter teases me and says, "Mom, you can't pass a weed without pulling it!" She's right, and that makes me happy. So by changing my attitude, I turned something I hated into something I enjoyed. It really was as simple as that.

The trick is to remember that it is possible to change your attitude right in the middle of a conversation or even an argument. Remembering to breathe deeply is the first step. Training yourself to simply "take a breath" when you feel any stress creep in is the key. The breath does two things: it clears your mind and it buys you time. Sending oxygen to the brain is important for clear thinking.

Taking that breath can become your trigger to tap into that ego or critical voice that is on alert to protect you. More often than not, you don't need the protection your ego would like you to employ. In recent years, I have experienced a technique that works on deep-seated beliefs. It is simply called Tapping.

Tapping is a combination of Eastern acupressure and Western psychology and can offer both physical and emotional pain relief. There are a number of practitioners who have researched and written about this technique and a few are listed in the resource list at the back of this book.

At times, I can change my attitude in a matter of seconds. If the issue is something that I am not highly invested in, it is simply a matter of remembering that I can change my attitude without feeling any sense of loss. It takes more effort if the issue is a long-held belief, or entails a personal sense of winning or losing my "case."

Being aware that the belief actually exists is the first step. Sometimes an issue is so deeply hidden, we don't even know we have a certain belief or a particular attitude toward something, nor do we know where it came from. My introduction to discovering where long-held beliefs originated came from my work with Pamela Bruner and Jack Canfield's work *Tapping Into Ultimate Success*. Mine had to do with money.

After making it through a difficult financial start in the first few years of marriage, I have always believed I would have enough money. "Enough" was the operative word. For most of my adult life I have lived in a thrifty fashion. I made "just enough" money to meet our needs. Sometimes the Universe would shower abundance on us but we would always make choices that put us back into the "just enough" category. Recently, I began to wonder why I believed just enough was a great attitude and belief to hold. Why not believe I could enjoy abundance? Last spring I decided to concentrate on attracting abundance into my life. Some interesting things have begun to appear. At this point, it is a work in progress. But I have changed my attitude from having "enough" to attracting financial abundance.

One thing I have learned is to be patient with the Universe. Sometimes, I am amazed at how quickly the Universe provides. Other times, a very long view is needed to connect the dots and understand that what I yearned for has already appeared in my life. Money is one of those areas for me.

Meeting Spiritual Entrepreneurs

Over the past few years, I have discovered some very talented, enlightened spiritual entrepreneurs who have helped shape my understanding of life and the ability to live with ease. At first, I was somewhat skeptical of people who conducted their practices on the Internet. Now I understand the Internet has provided many of us with avenues to reach like-minded people who, in the past, would have never met one another. In the introduction to this book I promised you a broad list of entrepreneurs. That list begins here with Pamela Bruner, coauthor of *Tapping Into Ultimate Success*.[1]

Pamela's work led me to a much deeper understanding of my emotional relationship with money and wealth. She introduced me to the Emotional Freedom Technique also called Emotional Freedom Tapping, Tapping or simply EFT. It wasn't long before I learned that Tapping was moving into the mainstream of the helping professions—psychology, medicine, pain therapy, weight management. A book and full-length documentary, created by Nick and Jessica Ortner, called *The Tapping Solution*[2] beautifully describes the process and how it can be used for everything from fears that hold you back to post-traumatic stress disorder among survivors of the genocide in Somalia and the Gulf Wars.

Nick & Jessica Ortner, and Pamela Bruner have successful Tapping practices that are available online. I have used their teachings and techniques to help me better understand what keeps me from enjoying abundance in my life.

Emotional Freedom Tapping (EFT) is one of the best methods I have found to rapidly "peel the onion" of my own experiences. Once I understand what has shaped an attitude that prevents me from living my highest and best life, it is not long before I can effectively change even lifelong attitudes. It doesn't have to take years of talk therapy, although there is a place for that, to work through life's roadblocks. Sometimes, one or two sessions of EFT can rocket you to a new understanding and acceptance of new attitudes.

As I said, I have always had enough-sometimes just barely enough, sometimes a generous enough amount of money. I eschewed the need for abundance. Why was that? It never occurred to me to ask that question. When I did, at Pamela's suggestion, I found my answer. Tapping on money and wealth, or more accurately, my inability to attract it, was my introduction to this effective modality.

Shifting a Long-Held Attitude
I was surprised to learn I had developed an understanding,

at a very early age, that wealthy people are often unhappy, selfish and mean. This was an attitude that came from my very limited exposure to a great aunt of mine, Eva Worcester, who was the wealthiest person I knew. She was a woman born on a farm in 1892. She was beautiful and married into a wealthy family. She had no children. She and her husband were not happy, and in the 1940s they divorced. She never remarried; and no one in the family was allowed to mention her ex-husband's name in her presence.

She lived in a beautiful home in a very chic community. She spent time in Palm Beach, Palm Springs and New England. After her divorce, she suffered a very deep depression and sought a cure through electroshock therapy. She also took up oil painting as a form of therapy. It turned out she was quite a gifted artist. She took lessons from an excellent teacher and, by the early 1960s, she had progressed to presenting a one-woman show in Paris of her still-life and landscape paintings of New England and Florida. In later years, she painted the desert of the American West.

When I visited her for several days each summer, I felt like a princess. Her house was the largest house I could imagine. I always had my choice of the Blue Room, the Green Room or the Peach Room when I stayed with her. All were beautifully decorated. She played the concert grand piano in her living room and encouraged me to sing. She helped me memorize poems and taught me to shake hands when I was introduced to her friends. She set up play dates for me to meet her friends' children. It was all magical.

Beneath the beautiful and entitled lifestyle I saw, I heard the adults in my life tell a different story. Aunt Eva had no children. After my paternal grandmother died, my father and his brother were her closest relatives. Since she had no nieces to care for her, it fell to my mother to answer the calls when she needed something or was ill. I remember several times when my mother would come home in tears after spending the day doing Aunt Eva's bidding. She treated my mother as if she was a servant. Her words and actions were often thoughtless and sometimes cruel. Aunt Eva was a miserable, unhappy woman who died alone. The only difference I could discern between her and the rest of my family was her money and the fact that the adults seemed to tolerate her, but were often hurt by her words and actions. As a child, I deduced it must have been the excess money and lack of children that made her so unhappy. They seemed to be the only things I could see that were different. Does that make any sense as an adult? No, of course not. But my childhood attitude followed me into adulthood. I didn't even have a conscious awareness of that attitude. But I now understand that it controlled much of my life where money was concerned.

Although I experienced abundance in other areas of my life – love, joy, meaningful work, faith; subconsciously, I was not interested in having an abundance of money if it meant I would not have love, happiness, joy and kindness in my life. I made choices according to my own subconscious belief. It wasn't that I didn't want more. I simply never had the desire to acquire more.

Furthermore, it seemed that more people entered my life who had money, but weren't happy. This added to my subconscious belief, that wealthy people weren't very kind. Being happy and kind are two things I hold dear and I did not want to be without them. The message from my childhood was not only clear, but it was being reinforced time and again. People who have money are not happy. I didn't know I had this belief until I began Pamela Bruner's course, "Tapping Into Ultimate Success." Some of the earliest worksheet notes from that course show my personal reflections as I tapped through my money blocks.

There it was, plain as day. What I learned as a young child was front and center in my adult beliefs about money. It would be dangerous to have more than I needed. I might not be happy or nice to others, so it was better to have only enough. Of course that makes no rational sense, but these beliefs come from an ego that has the innocence of a child and is simply trying to protect me. The tapping exercises exposed the faulty wiring from my childhood and opened me up to a deep desire to embrace abundance.

This book is about breathing, but there are additional modalities in the world of personal transformation that assist us in creating healthy, constructive, new attitudes that I will share with you throughout the book. When I do, I will direct you to an online workbook where you can find a short description of the method and online contact information to research any models you might find interesting.

Sometimes deep-seated beliefs can be helpful. It seems I have always had two things I believed in. One was that I could live through whatever "it" was, no matter how difficult or painful it might be at the time. The second was I could love myself even when I couldn't imagine anyone else would. I believe both of those things are attitudes I choose to hold. I can make myself believe them, because I can control my attitude even when I can't control anything else.

Do Your Deeply Held Beliefs Support You?
What deeply held belief do you have that might be standing in the way of living your highest and best life? Does it have to do with love, money, career, self-worth, creativity, health, moral fiber, happiness, body image, success? The list goes on and on, you choose your issue(s). Usually, you can tell when an issue causes you to feel stuck in your life. It will be something that has stopped you from achieving your goals over and over again.

If you would like to try tapping right now, I invite you to go to _www.skrcoaching.com_ where I will take you through an introductory tapping experience. In it you will have an opportunity to explore a particular area that may be blocking you from living your highest and best life.

Don't be surprised if you have an "aha" or two. Sometimes it takes a few tries to "tap" into your deeper emotions, but keep at it. It's worth it. Begin by breathing deeply and centering yourself. Relax and let go of any preconceived notion you may have of what this experience will bring. You can return to this exercise as often as you wish. It is a resource for you to use.

It is important for me to remember my attitude comes from within. It comes from what I call my essence or "Spirit." Your attitude comes from inside you, from your "Spirit." I invite you to join me in the next chapter on my spiritual journey. Take a deep cleansing breath and let's begin the journey.

Chapter 3

A Spiritual Journey

E very journey begins wherever you are. Right here, right now we take our first step, drive our first mile, and breathe the first breath on our journey. So whether you have been in touch with your spirit for years, or you have no idea what your spirit is, I invite you to take this step.

When I write about spirit, I am referring to the essence of who you are. This has nothing to do with religion. Your first step is to think back, way back to your early life. Early life experiences can provide clues as to why you feel what you feel today. They can also help you understand what you feel about yourself in the world, your place, your power or lack of it, and your understanding of how the world works.

Some folks spend years in psychotherapy rehashing the experiences of their lives. It is helpful to look at your past history. For the purposes of this book we will move along a bit faster. How? Well, **you have all the answers**. What you need are the questions. After all, no one else has lived your life. Your life, what you remember, is your story. It is a reflection of yourself. Your story is not like anyone else's story. If you would like proof of this, simply ask your siblings what they remember about certain family events. No siblings of your own? Ask your friends and their siblings a few questions. You are unlikely to hear the same memories from them. That is because our memories are not fact based, but feeling based. We think they are based on the exact moment we have an experience. But in reality, every previous experience we have ever had and our combined understanding of those experiences influence our understanding of that moment.

Part of the reason our stories differ is because our memories carry our own personal perspective of the situation. The things that were important to you may not be the same exact things that were important to someone else. The experiences you brought to that memory were unique. Your perspective is just that, yours. If you change your perspective, you may redefine your own life stories. Some practitioners refer to this as re-framing. It is a valuable tool.

We change every day. As we grow up, our bodies change shape. Throughout life our bodies grow, mature, age, decline and die on our human journey. Our perspective changes constantly. People who are aware of this are more likely to accept something new as possible. Why? Because they can look back and see how their opinions have changed over time. Those changes don't mean we lied about our truth in the past; it means we have simply learned something new that changes our understanding and our perspective. In fact, this ability to accept a changing perspective is a mechanism we use to heal our emotions.

Our physical bodies use this ability to change, to heal from an injury. When a wound occurs, our body rallies its forces to form a scab. The scab heals and we may be as good as new, or we may have a scar. That scar has changed our body. Even without a visible scar, that wound has altered our life experience. Your body is still your body and it continually transforms, so do your mind and your life.

Spiritual Stirrings

Our spirits are waiting for our minds and bodies to catch up and understand that we each have the resources to recover and move on. In this chapter, I have mentioned your body, your mind and your spirit. I have confidence that you are familiar and comfortable with the first two. Your spirit, however, might be a bit sketchier in your understanding of yourself. Often we hear people talk about having a spiritual experience. I believe they see themselves as primarily a human body with a mind having a spiritual experience. But what if ...

"We are spirits having a human experience." That's right. What if you saw yourself as a spirit – now and always? As a Spirit you have chosen to have a human experience. Imagine the wonder of your Spirit having a chance to play in a human body with five senses experiencing taste, touch, sight, smell and sound! But we plan to use those senses for a specific purpose.

When I use the term "Spirit" I am referring to the essence of your being. In my understanding of life we are, as French philosopher Pierre Teilhard de Chardin is quoted, "spirits having a human experience." In other words, we are not first and foremost physical beings, but we take on our physical bodies to live out our spiritual purpose.

I did not come to this understanding lightly. I lived my life much as most middle class Americans. I thought of myself as human first, for most of my six decades of life. Aware that my body wasn't all there is, I thought the rest was my mind or my thoughts. That pretty well summed up my total understanding of life. Raised with a Midwestern mainstream liberal Protestant faith, I felt there was more than I could see. I grew into a strong faith that I believed I chose. I didn't understand faith as another part of myself, but actually separate from me altogether something some humans believe in and others don't. I always felt very lucky to have what I thought of as faith. I saw faith as a gift given to all, some choose to cultivate their faith, while others let it lay fallow.

It was only as I looked at my life in the rear-view mirror that I began to see and feel there was something more than body and mind. Often I heard the word "spirit," but its meaning was vague. Spirit usually referred to the Christian concept of Trinity – Father, Son and Holy Spirit. Depending on context outside of religion, it meant either something in my mind or my "heart." I never thought of spirit as my essence. I thought of it as an emotion, perhaps a bit like love.

My perspective changed when I first heard the Teilhard quote. Hearing that I might think of myself "as a spirit having a human experience" shifted everything for me. Suddenly, I was not constrained by the physical. I could look back on my life and understand for the first time what part I played. I could understand that, although genetics played a part in my physical body, those genes did not affect my spirit. My spirit predated my genetic makeup! I wasn't only a scientific amalgamation of my mother and father.

If this is the first time you have thought of such a description of spirit, I encourage you to take some time with the idea. Spend some time pondering what it means to think of yourself as being a spirit. What did you come into the world with that maybe your siblings didn't? Do you have a special talent for something? Is there a passion you have or an ability that you have easily developed? Maybe you have always been afraid of something or have a hesitation to try things that others are just naturally able to do.

Have you ever heard of someone being referred to as "an old soul"? They don't look old; in fact the person could even be a child. Maybe they or you have been called "wise beyond your years." You know, the student in your graduating class who was a serious student, always thoughtful, able and well adjusted. The one who was poised in any situation. I like to think of those people as souls or spirits who have been here before. They didn't have to "start from scratch." They already knew a bit about human life and how to navigate this physical plane.

What Do You Know?

When I first became aware of this notion, it explained something I had been teaching for years which I called - What Do You Know? I later learned it began as the Four Stages of Competence.[3] It was originally used to describe the different steps we go through as we learn something new. However, I used it to describe the different ways we know certain things.

There are four types of knowing:

What you know you know – You are conversant in this topic; you may have studied it or practiced it. You are comfortable using this knowledge or skill. You have developed confidence in your ability around this topic.

What you know you don't know – You know you haven't learned this. You haven't read or studied or practiced some specific skill. For example, I know I am not a brain surgeon. I wouldn't attempt it. This is obvious to me.

What you don't know you don't know – This is the "sticky wicket." This is where the danger lies – when we run into something we have no knowledge, experience or understanding of and, therefore, have no idea we even need to know about it. When a teacher begins to berate a child for not completing a homework assignment or remembering to bring a permission slip, the teacher assumes she/he knows the child's circumstances and holds the child at fault, only to learn the child's father suffered a heart attack the night before. Or it could be a situation where you assume someone is ignoring you and you become irritated. Moments later you see them using sign language to communicate, because they are hearing impaired.

What you don't know you know – This is something you simply know – you haven't studied it, you haven't done it before, you may not have ever seen it, but you just know what to do and how to do it. You can't explain why; you may not have even thought about it. I believe these are the areas where our gifts reside. The person who picks up a violin and plays it without training, the person who speaks with ease and confidence with no training, the person who masters a sport the first or second time out. When asked, "How did you know?" The response is often, "I don't know. I have just always known."

What does this have to do with Spirit? I believe the "What you don't know you know" may be what we bring with us into our current human existence. We don't have to learn it, we just **know**. Do you have anything that falls into that category in your life? Maybe it's your ability to parent or nurture others. Maybe it's the gift of music or intuition, a knack for public speaking or cooking or healing. Whatever it is, honor it and use it for your highest and best good. It is truly a gift you are bringing into this world. It is equipment you will use on your spiritual journey.

When I speak of a Spiritual Journey, I am not referring to a particular event or time. I am referring to what academics would call a "body of work." My spiritual journey began when I, Susan, began. It is comprised of every opportunity I have taken to reach beyond the physical world and its rational knowledge. In other words, it is a compilation of my experiences, thoughts and insights that connect me to my own innate wisdom. The part of me that "knows" but has not "learned."

The Spiritual Journey Begins
If I had to choose a particular moment when a spiritual, as opposed to a religious, switch began to turn on, it would be

when I entered a National Day of Prayer event in my small church in Troy. A little background might be helpful here. Troy is a very culturally diverse community – ethnically, racially, and religiously. A member from the Hindu community asked to be included in the annual city program and was denied. She was told it was a "Christian-only" event. A few of Troy's religious leaders decided this outrage would not be tolerated. If we couldn't all worship together on the National Day of Prayer at the City Hall, everyone would be invited to come together at another place. Our little church was offered.

I walked into the sanctuary where I worshiped every Sunday and heard an Indian band playing sitars and looked around at the beautiful diversity of faces and clothing. I was struck with a thought. All of the divisions we humans create are just that – created by our thoughts. If we can sit in Troy, Michigan, USA, North America, Earth, Milky Way, the Universe and join together in a loving and peaceful gathering, why couldn't the whole world do the same thing?

That was a giant step in my Spiritual Journey. The ground had been tilled for me over the previous years, when a spiritual formation group formed at my church. During our discussions, everything was acceptable. We had members with firmly fixed traditional Christian beliefs, and we had agnostics and everything in between. Seeds had been planted that allowed real exploration of my faith. From there I began to read a series of books. I encourage you to begin to read authors who are exploring topics that pique your interest. I found that one book led to another. First, I was interested in how the Christian, Jewish and Islamic faiths intersected. I was hungry to understand what the Abrahamic faiths really were. What did they have in common, what were their divisions and why? My first read was *Abraham* by Bruce Feiler.[4]

Next came *The Faith Club*[5] written by three New York women who began to meet after 9/11 to learn about one another's faith – Christianity, Judaism and Islam. I would hear about a book or mention to someone I was really trying to understand the divisions created around the world by our differing cultures and religions. People would offer titles I might like. Many were best sellers like *Reading Lolita in Tehran,*[6] *The Kite Runner,*[7] *Three Cups of Tea,*[8] *Stones into Schools,*[9] *The Red Tent*[10] and *Nine Parts of Desire.*[11] Reading wasn't enough. I wanted hands-on experiences with other faiths and cultures. They were right in my backyard; all I had to do was make an effort.

Soon I was telling members of my church that I would be taking a sabbatical and visiting other churches for a year. From January through December, I visited a wide variety of Christian churches. I visited the local synagogue for Shabbat services and other events throughout the year. One of the most enlightening memories I have from that year was visiting a mosque open house where a Jewish friend and I were warmly welcomed by the Imam. We learned more about Islamic history, food, worship, and culture in that one-day than by reading books for a year. There was a celebration at the local Hindu Temple, where I learned a Hindu temple serves more as a community center than a house of worship. I visited "big box" churches and tiny houses of worship. I visited two Unitarian churches, which were vastly different from each other. I visited a church that was more a family business than a house of worship. I visited old churches like the Old Mariner's Church in Detroit, which was built for mariners in 1842. Transient sailors were not welcome at other churches because they were thought to be unsavory characters. That visit offered insight into historic attitudes in a Christian tradition. I attended lectures that included representatives from a broad range of faiths. I learned about the Baha'i Faith. A friend gifted me with an encyclopedia of the world's religions, which was very helpful. With each visit I learned more about the role religious attitudes play in our lives.

When that part of my Spiritual Journey concluded, I happily returned to my home church. People asked me, "What did you learn?" I thought hard about how I would honestly answer that question. My reply was the same then as it is today, "The major religions seem to share a philosophy that caring for one another is important. The Golden Rule is woven through each of them. I also learned that all religion is flawed because it was created by man." By that I mean humans have a very bad habit of believing what they think is the truth. It is only their version of the truth. When their truth becomes a religion, their human flaws are woven into the religion. So whether it was the early Christians putting their spin on what they believed Jesus meant to say, based on their culture at the time, or the strict Islamist of today interpreting the Koran, with their current cultural understanding, it all boils down to humanity's hubris, including my own. Religious rules are generally a result of the cultural times in which they were laid down.

Having told people that religion is flawed, I would often be asked, "Why do you attend church?" The answer was obvious to me.

I am a person who loves to be involved in what I refer to as a community of believers. I need to be with people who believe it is important to love all people, to take responsibility for ourselves and to help others. I raised my daughter to be happy and "do good." That was not a grammatical error – I really meant I hoped she would go out into the world and do good works at every opportunity. I believe it is one of the most important ways to feed our souls. To feed my soul I attend church and generally I try to "do good" in my little corner of the world.

That said, I returned to the Presbyterian Church after my year of experiential learning with an understanding that I no longer believed the creeds of the church. I realized I hadn't believed them for a long time. But they felt comfortable before. Now they began to chafe at my soul and my mind. But

I truly loved all the people I learned, served and worshiped with on Sundays. I was unwilling to give them up. So, for several years I continued to be very active in the church, all the while knowing I was growing apart from my childhood religious roots.

As fate would have it, I would be moving to a new community that gave me an opportunity to explore another spiritual possibility. About a year after my husband and I moved to Holt, Michigan. I visited the Unitarian Universalist Church of Greater Lansing. As soon as I heard the welcome, "Whoever you are, wherever you are on your Spiritual Journey and whomever you love, you are welcome," I knew I was home. At last I had found a place without creeds, without pronouns to stumble over, and a genuine respect for each person's understanding of their own life and spiritual experience. Now I was really free to experience spirit in a variety of ways.

Learning about the Spirit of Energy

I was introduced to the spirit of energy by world-renowned energy healer, Donna Eden through her book *Energy Medicine*.[12] Donna and her husband, David Feinstein, are a power couple in more ways than one. She is an Energy Healer and he is actively researching and teaching Energy Psychology. Both of these areas of insight are quickly moving into the mainstream of the healing arts. Eden Energy practitioners are being trained across the county.

We have all felt chills at one time or another – completely unrelated to room temperature. You may have rubbed your hands together quickly and pulled apart slowly to feel "something" between your palms. As I learned more about our bodies' energy systems, I was amazed at how natural my new understanding and experience of my own energy felt.

Sometimes I am aware of my energetic connection to the Universe. It occurs without my intention. I can feel a tingling sensation of energy that feels exciting. It may come when I see a sunset or sunrise, a beautiful vista, my grandchild coming to me with a loving word or kiss, my husband reaching out to hold my hand as we walk along. I may recognize a feeling of connectedness that comes when words flow with wisdom and knowledge from my mouth without any preparation. Often, I feel an energetic swirl in a room where I am meeting with people who become excited by the creative work we are doing. That energy is available to each of us 24/7. Like all things Spiritual, all we need to do is invite the spirit in. Spirit is not intrusive. It is polite and waits for a request and invitation, an expressed desire.

Inviting Spirit into My Life
When I am in a quandary and need reassurance or direction, I ask my Spirit for answers. This is what this book is all about, accessing that Inner Wisdom which we all possess.

My belief is that humankind is connected, and we have access to an unlimited pool of wisdom. All we have to do is ask. Wisdom waits for us to request help. Wisdom doesn't intrude on our human existence unless we extend an invitation. When I began to play with this idea, I was surprised, to say the least. I had been practicing my technique of breathing in deeply, slowly and mindfully. Holding my breath for an extra moment. Then exhaling, slowly and deeply. While I was breathing in this way, I silently asked my Spirit where a particular fear was coming from. The answer was immediately present. It was so clear and so "right on!" I was surprised I hadn't known it all along. I have heard people refer to this connection to spirit described as "a hit," a voice, or simply knowing. For me, it is the knowing. I might take a deep in-breath, focusing on asking Spirit a particular question. Often, before I form the words in my mind and say them to myself, the answer is present. I "know." At first I didn't trust it. Before long, I realized the distrust was coming from my ego trying to protect me from what it doesn't understand.

I continued to ask Spirit questions often and receive answers – some more veiled than others, and not always right away. It wasn't long before I realized that I had been accessing Spirit for years, but had not realized it. At times when I would know I was going to speak publicly, or attend a meeting in which I would be called upon to provide information or create something I had no experience in, I would silently ask for help. Sometimes, I would ask that the right words come from my mouth, or for insight into a difficult challenge or question. At times I would ask for access to the person who could best help me. Always the answers came. I can't explain it other than to say we all have access to an incredible wisdom. If we could learn to ask, to listen and to trust, our lives would be so much easier.

When my requests are fulfilled, I am in awe. Sometimes, I am answering a question with information I have never read or experienced, but I know it is better than anything I could have created on my own. Spirit is flowing. It is the best feeling in the world! I call that speaking from my heart. Often when I write, I am surprised to see what my fingers are typing. I am not planning what will be written. I may have a topic in mind, but where it will go or what will be said is not planned. When I have asked Spirit for help with a particular topic and I am ready to let go of the control, the words and ideas flow with ease.

On the other hand, when I try to control the outcome, the process can be messy, challenging and fraught with wanting to meet my own needs. It always takes more time and effort than if I simply connect to Spirit and allow the wisdom to come in and through me.

Have You Met Your Spirit?

How do you describe that part of you that is not physical (your body) and not mental (your mind), but the essence of who you are? What role does that essence play in your life? Does it support your life dreams?

Is it the seat of where your dreams are created?

Does it support you with guidance, wisdom, information, anything?

Please take time to consider your answers to these questions. Take your time. There is no hurry. The answers may come now or years from now. But, if asked, they will present themselves.

Whether this is the first step in your own Spiritual Journey, or one of many steps you have already taken, questions like these can provide intriguing ideas.

Let me share how this understanding of life perspective changes my story and how shifting your perspective might change yours in the next chapter.

Breathe

Chapter 4

Looking at Life in the Rearview Mirror

A t 19, a junior in college, I married. Bob and I had met in a modern dance group called Orchesis. He was a senior and I was a freshman. It was not love at first sight, but he danced beautifully. Slowly I began to enjoy his sense of humor, his artistic talents and his generous spirit. His six-foot three-inch frame and curly hair didn't hurt. That spring, we decided to choreograph a dance together for the Orchesis Concert and we didn't have much time to prepare. Over one twenty-four hour period, we danced and choreographed our work for 18 hours. It was an exhausting and bonding experience. Our dancing became a metaphor for our relationship for the next 15 years.

Over the next few weeks, we became a couple. Our time together was filled with fun and dance; our time apart was spent studying and attending classes. We were falling in love. Eighteen months later, Bob graduated from college and began his Master's degree work. I had transferred to Michigan State University and we were married. From my perspective, the marriage was very happy. But life dealt us a blow even before we returned from our week-long Florida honeymoon. He received a notice to appear in Detroit for a military physical. This was during the Vietnam War and the draft was very active.

Eighteen weeks after our wedding, he headed to Fort Knox, Kentucky for basic training and a two-year Army commitment. I prayed he wouldn't be sent to Vietnam. I was a twenty-year-old bride, in college, left with a variety of loans, rent, and utilities to pay, and completely alone. The first thing I did was find a job, and then a second one. With two jobs, attending classes and studying, my time was filled. After five months of various types of training, Bob received orders for Ft. Leonard Wood in Waynesville, Missouri. I joined him and, finally, I felt like we could start our married life. But the Army had other ideas, and within three months he received orders for Korea. At least it wasn't Vietnam, but it was far away and a hardship tour, which meant I wouldn't be going. I had to stay in Missouri, hundreds of miles from family and friends, struggling to pay the bills. I had dropped out of school to join Bob in Missouri. Now he was gone, and I was there – alone.

Needless to say, the first two years of our marriage included many ups and downs. We were apart for months at time. A severe strain was put on our marriage both financially and emotionally. Two years later, as we returned to civilian life, I completed my college degree and he settled into his career. In our fifth year of marriage, we welcomed our daughter into this world. From my perspective, our life was as perfect as it could be. We had the Cape Cod house, our beautiful daughter, a dog, two cars and we loved each other. It was the 1970's version of the American dream. However, in year thirteen, my husband announced he no longer wanted to be married to me. He moved out and I eventually filed for divorce.

The events of the previous paragraph sets the stage for what came next.

The day he left, I was devastated. He had given me plenty of warning. The previous June, when I returned from two weeks of directing Girl Scout camp, a part of my job, Bob had changed. He was critical of me, demanding more time to pursue his community theatre activities and playing sports. I was working full time with evening meetings, and we had our daughter to care for as well. As I look back, I realized there was a seismic shift in our relationship. It simply began to deteriorate. Over the summer, it got worse. I began to doubt everything I understood about our relationship. By September I asked if there was someone else. He said there was, but wouldn't disclose anything. We went to a counselor, which didn't help me, but I think it solidified his desire to be free. This wasn't the first challenge we had faced, but in the past we had decided we wanted to stay married. I believed he would change his mind this time, too. We had talked about it and I even went with him to help pick out an apartment. I knew there was another woman, but I never knew who she was. That is my story. That is the story I believed to be true and told for years. He no longer wanted to be married to me. He was leaving. I filed for divorce to improve my odds that a judge would allow me to maintain custody of our daughter.

One of the things that happens when you are blind-sided with a loss is that you believe you no longer have a future. The future you envisioned with this other person, or job, or dream, is no longer a part of your picture. Unless you really do live in the moment, the future you imagine is as real as the present. You imagine paying off your car loan. That will be in the future, but the payment you make today will help you achieve the future you desire. Your child is seven years old and you picture the future of her graduation from high school when you and your husband proudly watch her receive her diploma. There are so many dreams that disappear when a loss of a loved one occurs. At that moment you cannot imagine replacing those dreams with new ones. I know I couldn't.

I felt the loss of my marriage erased not only my future, but everything I put into my marriage and life. Everything that created my understanding of my place in life and my future as a wife was just ... gone. This led to an extended period of grief. On the weekends when my husband had our daughter, I would wander around the house in my pajamas for most of the day. I remember the first New Year's Eve when I was completely alone. The next day would mark the first anniversary of my husband moving out. That day, there were moments filled with sadness, deep sadness. Sometime around midnight I realized I had lived through a whole year of "being left." What had I done with that year?

During those twelve months, I had attended the Creative Problem Solving Institute and opened myself to a whole new way of thinking. Amy and I had taken a camping trip from Michigan through Illinois, Iowa, Nebraska, Colorado, Wyoming, South Dakota and Minnesota by ourselves. I pulled a small tent camper and felt free and excited. We returned home to continuing financial challenges, but I was no longer wearing my pajamas all day! I was working in a career I loved. The bills were being paid, even though finances were always tight. But I was putting one foot in front of the other and I continued to breathe – through an entire year.

It was during that year and the next that I began to create a different future. I went to graduate school. I redefined myself as a single parent. I looked forward to successfully completing my M.B.A. and starting a new career. At some point my perspective shifted from "being left" to being a survivor, and I added new chapters to my story.

I learned to single parent. It wasn't always easy. There were financial worries. But when I knew what I wanted – that second step to the change process – I learned I could always achieve it. It might take time and hard work. It might feel challenging, but never impossible. I learned to make every penny count. When my daughter was having difficulty learning her multiplication tables, I devised a plan that would make it possible for her to practice without having a meltdown. I would take her to the corner diner for her favorite grilled cheese sandwich and chocolate milk. I couldn't afford to buy dinner for both of us, so I would order only for her. While we waited for her dinner we would go over the multiplication tables. I knew she wouldn't pitch a fit in pubic (thank goodness) and I thought she never noticed I wasn't eating. Years later, she asked why I never ate when we went out. By that time she was an adult who could multiply, and I told her the truth. The one unchangeable during this entire time was my love for my daughter. She was my anchor and my raison d'être.

Now when I look back at the divorce I can see it did not devastate me; it simply opened me up to new experiences. Was there pain? Yes, deep pain and feelings of loss. Were my feelings at the time real? Absolutely. But that was not the end of my story. It was only one chapter in my life, not the entire book. I have learned that what looks like a door slammed in my face is nothing more than a directional stop sign inviting me to change course and proceed. But to get this far I had to remember to BREATHE.

My story continues today, as I share my life with Michael, my wonderful husband of almost three decades. I have learned what love really feels like. Could I have predicted I would meet my perfect mate? No. But having lived through that experience I can add to my story a belief that out of loss can come something different and often much better. My perspective changed, my life changed. I reframed my story.

There were so many people who helped us through those very lean years. My parents helped pay for tutoring, dance lessons and summer camp. Bob chipped in, too. Amy's school lunches were subsidized, and I was never embarrassed to ask that she be included in the government program. When I needed a loan for the divorce, my sister & brother-in-law helped out. I paid them and they assured me the money was always there if I needed it. I did need it again later and was grateful they so willingly helped. The angels in our lives looked just like everyday people. I learned to ask for help when I needed it. Pride was not a commodity that was particularly useful at this time in my life. I believed I could do what I needed and wanted to do. I would find the resources either by earning or borrowing or through the good will of others.

As I look back, I am amazed at what I was able to accomplish during those four years with the help of so many friends and my loving family. I learned to live into my future by moving forward. Remember, we learned that knowing the first step toward the change we want in our lives leads to the next step, and the next, always moving forward toward the future we want.

Speaking of looking to the future, one of the best lessons I learned has to do with making lists. When Bob and I went to see a marriage counselor we were asked to make a list of everything we wanted in a spouse. When we shared our lists, Bob's list and mine had nothing in common. I worked hard on my detailed list, considering the type of person, his family, the importance of mutual respect and love we would share. I stuck the list in a dresser drawer after I shared it with the counselor. I'll come back to that list in Chapter 11.

I mention the list here, because it has become apparent to me that the act of writing down what I desire is one way to take the second step in the change process – knowing the outcome you desire. Making a list defines the outcome you want to achieve. It is almost like magic.

In Chapter 11, I mention another list. One I made on my first day at Chrysler. I listed the accomplishments I would achieve over the next five years, including promotions and pay raises along with the dates I would achieve them. Every one of the intentions was fulfilled. But I never added to the list; I left before my sixth year ended. Do you suppose it was because my list ended with year five?

More recently, I discovered a list Michael and I wrote not long after we were married and had moved into our Troy home. It was a wish list of everything we wanted to add to our home and yard. The list was extravagant. We envisioned a professional landscape design coming to fruition, new flooring and a gutted and remodeled kitchen and family room. All of these things were vastly out of our reach at the time. When we moved from that home to our current one, I discovered the old list. We had completed every single item on the list over the 27 years we lived in Troy! I could hardly believe my eyes. Over the years the projects had taken place organically, not because we had a grand design – or was it?

I share these stories to illustrate how very important it is to dream about what you want and write those dreams down. You don't have to post them on your bathroom mirror. My experience is that the simple act of recording them increases the likelihood you will achieve what you record.

This chapter has been about looking at some great disappoint- ments in my life, unexpected challenges and losses. None of them killed me. The sadness didn't last forever. The grieving passed. Over time I have realized that the lessons I learned were valuable. I added tools that would help me live a happier, more fulfilling life. I may have even learned enough to believe the lessons learned were worth the pain.

The dissolution of my first marriage gutted me. But the new guts that grew were stronger, wiser and better equipped to help me love my future. I learned to be braver than I even knew was possible. I learned to be a single parent. I grew as an individual in ways I might never have known possible if I had always been part of a couple. Remember, I was only 19 when I married. My first attempt to be a single individual was at the age of 34. Looking at my life in the rearview mirror, I realize the challenges in my life have often been when my greatest growth took place.

Living as a single parent was hard. Living as a single parent on an income that made my child eligible for subsidized breakfasts and lunches illustrates the level of poverty we experienced. Having a difficult time finding employment after graduation because of age discrimination in the university career center was disheartening. Not one of those experiences killed me. In fact, I learned from each one. I think of the hard stuff as fertilizer that helps create a more beautiful future.

What do I mean by that?

I mean you don't have to love or even like all of your life experiences. I certainly don't. But thinking differently about the parts that bring you sadness, loss, frustration, fear and even grief will free your mind to see those experiences as valuable lessons when viewed in your own rearview mirror.

As you look back on your life, how might you reframe some of the disappointments you have experienced? Did the loss make space for something better? It's easy to get lost in how difficult it is to make your way into your better future. Don't stop there.

What experiences have you "learned through" to achieve the future you are living today? In other words, what life experiences changed your understanding of life in ways that changed how you are living your life today? Before you move on to the next chapter, take some time to think about this. Grab a pen and paper, or your laptop, and start making a list. Don't limit your list to your recent situation. Think back over your life from the time you can remember. What disappointments were there that turned out to be opportunities for growth or greater happiness?

If you are a cup-half-full thinker, you will have no trouble with the list once you get started. It may take a shift in your perspective. Your list will grow over time. If you tend to be a cup-half-empty thinker, this exercise may be a bit more challenging. If you are honest with yourself, you will find your list has some happy stories. Have those stories come from some seemingly unhappy event? Focus on those happy stories. Keep adding to your list as you think of new things. Change the list as your memories shift. Keep in mind: this is your list; this is your story; this is your life. You make the choices about how you will frame your story.

We draw to ourselves that upon which we focus. In the next chapter I will share an example of how true this is.

Breathe

Chapter 5

Be Careful What You Wish For

After 16 years of a successful partnership, my business partner Penny was retiring. She is six years older than I and was eligible to retire, according to the Federal Government. This had all been carefully planned, and I knew I was going to buy her out. All was good. Well, almost everything.

I just kept thinking I wish I could retire, too. Although I enjoyed the work I did, I was also looking forward to a time when my husband and I could spend more time together. We wanted to take longer cruises on the sailboat he had built 25 years before. I wanted to work in the garden, read and simply enjoy life. But it wasn't my time yet. So I just kept wishing and occasionally saying to close friends and family, "What I really want is to retire." I have not often been a person to wish my life away. I was the financial support for my family and I also knew I couldn't possibly have done what I did without my wonderful stay-at-home husband who took care of everything there. So I continued to work with no plans to retire until December 31, 2013.

I adjusted my schedule to suit my night owl tendencies. My staff handled the morning opening of the office and I often worked into the late evening hours to complete projects, write newsletters, and prepare for events. I had all the flexibility I wanted – I was my own boss. Of course, I never lost sight that my clients were really in the driver's seat, and I worked hard to please them. Day-to-day I had the flexibility most working people dream of. I usually worked about 50 hours a week and enjoyed most of it.

As I paid my former business partner each month, I wished I was the one who was retired and receiving payments instead of making them. Little did I know where that wishing would lead. I was about to create the reality I wished for — kind of.

What does it mean to create your own reality? Does it mean you can control everything in your life? Absolutely not. Does it mean that you wish for bad things to happen to you and that is why bad things happen? Again, no. What it does mean is that good things happen and bad things happen and neutral things happen. How you react to those things creates the reality you experience. To illustrate this idea, I will share a personal experience.

In this book's introduction, I shared one of my life crises. For 16 years, my company had served a non-profit client by providing day-to-day management of the organization, member recruitment, coordination of a variety of monthly programs and financial management. I served as Executive Director. We conducted fundraisers, wrote the monthly newsletter and all other membership communication, and steadily grew the organization from 40 members to more than 300. Every two or three years our "Letter of Agreement" was renegotiated. We were often publicly and privately thanked for the hard work we did to grow the organization and keep it on track. Over 16 years, this contract became a financially important one to us. It also took an extraordinary amount of our staff's resources. Although we also worked for Fortune 100 companies and conducted research projects for local municipalities and small businesses, those projects were of shorter duration, often several months. After the economic downturn began in Michigan in 2001, our automotive project work dwindled. At the same time, membership retention and recruitment in the non-profit sector became more challenging. The economic problems plaguing the auto industry were affecting us on every front. We were located in a city that was home to one of the Big Three U.S. auto companies and many of their suppliers were the members we served.

In the fall of 2008, I received feedback, which seemed sudden and unexpected from my standpoint. Some members of the Board of Directors were questioning the financial relationship the organization had with my company as well as the financial value of our work. My initial reaction was to take the criticism very personally. I had no idea why this was happening. First I was shocked, then angry. Months later I decided to sever the contractual relationship rather than allow the Board of Directors of the non-profit to end it. Losing this valuable client meant I would likely close the business, dissolve the corporation and "retire." Talk about actions coming from fear! My actions were driven by a fear that was so large I couldn't hear reason, even when I was presented with it.

My reality was that the members of the Board of Directors had decided our work was not equal to the value we were being paid. They wanted someone younger to manage the organization. They no longer valued what my staff and I had done for the past 16 years.

In truth, I had no idea what they were thinking. Although I talked with a number of board members over the 20 or so months from the original bombshell until the actual date the contract ended, I was unable to hear what was being said. My fear was so great there was little room for reason.

It wasn't that my ears weren't working; my brain was in distress mode. My "primitive brain" was in protection mode. I felt that I was being personally attacked and I felt terribly hurt. My brain was trying to offer protective advice – the kind of advice that didn't allow me to understand or hear other, both logical and loving advice when it was offered. The negative criticism was flying in all directions, from board members and from me. The only way to make it stop seemed to be to escape. So I did. I chose flight rather than fight. The part of my brain that is alert to danger, the amygdala, was in control.

I now realize my brain was remembering another time when something like this happened and it was going to protect me from a repeat performance! I often tell people this experience was as difficult as going through the divorce in 1981. At the time, I didn't understand how much that fear-filled experience was driving my 2009-2010 actions. I thought I was taking control by preparing to dissolve the relationship myself this time! I can see now that was not a particularly enlightened approach. At the time it felt like the only possible option available. I never thought to breathe! I didn't even know then that it would help. I couldn't seem to access any useful emotional tools to constructively approach the problem.

Who is in the Driver's Seat?
Let's take a look at who was in the Driver's Seat of my life during this period. To do that, there are five concepts that helped me discover how I created my own reality, and then recreated it.

The first concept is **All Actions are Driven by Love or Fear.** This is a concept taken from *A Course in Miracles*[13] scribed by Dr. Helen Schucman. Foregoing the religious nature of the course, I was so struck by this notion that I began to really pay attention to the actions of those around me as well as my own. I began to understand that anger, anxiety, frustration, disappointment, jealousy, sadness, shame, guilt, despair, envy, doubt, etc. are all expressions of fear. Likewise, compassion, admiration, joy, contentment, ease, fulfillment, pride, hope, peacefulness, exuberance, etc. are expressions of love. Although I have not attempted to prove that *all* actions come from love or fear, I have experienced enough examples that I am confident I can trace my own actions to one of those two states of being.

Taking that concept a step further, I ask, "What am I afraid of?" when I express myself in a negative way. Looking at the dissolution of my company I can see at least a few fears – loss of self-esteem and loss of income. How would I loose self-esteem? I pride myself on hard work and always providing value where money is concerned - my clients or mine. What I heard the client organization saying was my company was not delivering full value for the price we charged. That was the antithesis of everything I stand for. I felt my integrity was being called into question. If we weren't delivering, then they would have every right to cancel the contract. If the contract was cancelled, it was unlikely my business would survive in its current structure with the current economic environment. Fear was definitely in the driver's seat. Every day my thoughts circled around how I could prove my worth. This is the point at which I should have tried to slow down, take a deep breath and access the wisdom within; but I didn't remember to do that. My thoughts were clearly focused on "protecting myself from the enemy." My actions were coming from fear. The essence of who I am was overcome by my brain taking control and smothering my spirit. My ego took charge.

This brings us to the second concept – **Your Thoughts Direct Your Life**. Henry Ford is credited with saying, "Whether you think you can or you think you can't, you're right." I believe that is true. We attract what we think about and what we expect more often than not. For 20 months I moved from anger to fear through self-righteousness. That fear led me to submit a notification to the Board of Directors that TMD Consulting was terminating its agreement, effective 90 days hence. It was accepted, and we began to prepare for the closing of the company. This whole experience felt very much like the divorce I had gone through 29 years earlier – the sadness, anger and loss felt all too familiar. This time I was leaving. As I turned out the lights and locked the office door for the last time, I was exhausted and uncertain about what would come next for me professionally. Twenty years of my life's work was put into storage; furniture, files, copies of all of the projects we had created and delivered to our many clients over the years. Three days later my husband and I left to cruise the Great Lakes on our sailboat for five weeks.

I needed every moment of those five weeks to begin to recover. The first week I slept. I would wake long enough to prepare meals, but that was about all I could do. The second week I began to read and sit on the deck soaking up the healing warmth of the sun (with appropriate sunblock of course). By the third week I was really enjoying our time together and with friends we visited along the way. By the time we returned home from our vacation, I was rested and ready to consider facing the world. It would take at least another year before I would be able to comprehend what had really happened and for me to take responsibility for my part in the outcome.

The third concept is **Be Careful What You Wish For**. Do you remember what I was wishing for? I wanted to retire from the work I was doing so I could do what I yearned to do. Here I was retired, but it felt somewhat sad and empty. More truthfully it was I who felt sad and empty. I hadn't really expected or planned to retire early. I needed to work – or so I thought. I had not made the connection between wishing I could retire and closing my business in the worst economy since the Great Depression! That knowledge came a few years later. But here I was, experiencing exactly what

I had concentrated on and wished for – retirement and time to do what I wanted.

Have you ever thought you knew what might happen if you did something and then realized that, like a bad recipe, it didn't taste, smell or look like what you had in mind?

Well, there you have it.

As I said, I slept most of the time for the first week on our boat. The second week I began to enjoy having the freedom to be on an extended vacation. The next three weeks I reveled in the beauty of nature, staying with friends for several days along the way and returning to a life that did not include 50-hour workweeks. During this time I found myself fighting the "demons." Often, whether I was awake or asleep, I was creating arguments defending my worth. Over time those thoughts became less and less frequent. About 18 months later, when I finally realized I had gotten what I wished for, they stopped altogether.

The fourth concept is to **Transform Your Demons into Your Teachers.** The "demons" consisted of my memories of conversations, real and imagined. It was when I lay down to sleep that the real show began. I wound my way through things I should have said or actions I should have taken to "show them!" Then I would stop and remind myself I was better off now. But it didn't feel better. It felt frustrating and unfinished. What was it I really wanted? How could I come to a center of calm? What was I missing? What did I need to do to be done with these feelings of failure? Why couldn't I just move on?

After months of this, I was sitting in church one Sunday and the minister asked us to imagine forgiving someone for something unforgivable. What would that feel like?

I knew exactly whom I would choose – in fact I knew several somebodies I would choose to forgive. I really meant that. I was exhausted from being angry, unhappy and hurt. I wanted to move on, but how? This was my opportunity. Maybe I could just say to myself, "I forgive you." I could also forgive each person I believed had treated me unfairly. Over the next several days, as I worked through the list in my head, I experienced a little lifting of the burden I had been carrying. I literally felt lighter as I thought of each person I had been arguing with in my head and thought about the part I had played and what I might have done differently. I considered how my responses had been so focused on defense that it never occurred to me to listen for any lesson I might have received from those who had tried to help.

Now don't misunderstand me. I am not saying that anyone else in each of the hurtful encounters I experienced, from the moment I was sent from the Board meeting until I locked the office door for the last time, set out to teach me anything or to hurt me. In truth I have no idea what their intentions were. Only they would know, and that would be their reality. What I am saying is I was able, over time, to look at what occurred in a very different light. In other words, I created my own reality from my own beliefs about what was happening. If I created my unhappy reality, could I also shift it?

How did I shift from being a victim to living the life I have created of freedom and joy? By processing (or discussing) what was happening to me in conversations with friends and family. I meditated. I learned about myself. I chose to move from surviving to thriving. I wanted to feel that I could do something very productive with the rest of my life. To do that I needed to give up being a victim and become my own hero. I needed to create my own reality.

The fifth concept is **Allow Your Best Self to Move Into the Driver's Seat**. I didn't enjoy being a victim. At some point, I knew I could not find my first healthy step in the change process (see Chapter 1) until I could forgive the people who were involved in the reality I didn't like. I didn't need to forgive them in person. In fact, they didn't even need to know I was thinking about them. But I needed to forgive them for myself.

It was about a year after I closed the office. All of the furniture and papers were still in storage, but I was ready to move on. As I sorted through each paper and project file, I had time to think. I was alone, sitting in the sunshine with the door open on the storage unit when it struck me. I no longer had to work a traditional workweek. THAT, I had yearned for. When my business partner retired, I so wished I could too. I even told people my wish was to retire, but I knew I needed to keep working until I was old enough to receive Social Security. That was my reality.

So, work I did – long and hard. I enjoyed the work, but I wanted more freedom. I wanted to be able to spend time with my husband and my daughter and her family. I wanted to live closer to my grandchildren. The clock kept ticking; and three years after my business partner retired, I found myself retired ahead of time! But at first it felt more like I was shoved out. It took me a little over two years to realize all the turmoil and pain, sadness and loss, anger and fear were a result of the universe giving me exactly what I had asked for – a way to retire. I was given a way out without realizing that was what had happened. With the bright summer sun bathing me in warmth and light, I suddenly understood my new reality. I had been given the retirement I wanted.

How can I take credit for creating such a difficult exit for myself? Back in the first chapter I told you "our spirits are waiting for our minds to catch up." This is a perfect example. My spirit knew what my heart wanted and found an opportunity to help me get there. Unfortunately my primitive brain, the part that tries hard to protect me based on limited data, didn't understand that. It decided the Board's actions were harmful and I should be afraid, instead of embracing them and planning for a welcome change. If I had known then to breathe into my own wisdom, I might have saved myself, and those who cared for me, a good deal of grief. As it was, I barely breathed and struggled greatly. I was full of fear about the future. I didn't even know I had wisdom within. My wisdom was patiently waiting for my brain to discover its existence.

As the breadwinner of our family, losing my income looked like a disaster. Instead of having an opportunity to finish what I believed was the correct timing for my exit from the nine-to-five world, I felt "thrown under the bus." If I had known then what I know now, it would not have taken almost four years to accept the ramifications of the very first conversation that raised questions about my company. I can now imagine a scenario where I would have presented the facts (I actually did that) and when it became clear it was time for a change. I would have carefully explained the steps I was willing to take, described an exit strategy that would have been in my highest and best good, and taken the next step on my path to change. In fact, had I understood more about my own internal wisdom I might have consulted it. I might have been more circumspect in my reactions. I might have even chosen a different path. But I didn't know, understand or consult my inner-wisdom. I experienced all the human emotions associated with unexpected change that feels out of control. If only I had known then how to Breathe into Wisdom.

I feel certain there are many of us who are unable or unwilling to take that deep breath, and ask Wisdom, "What will be in my highest and best good? What should be my next step?" Even if we remember to ask, the next absolutely necessary step is to listen patiently and quietly for the answer.

How will you know when you have received the answer? That's the challenge because there are so many ways you might experience this. I hear the words in my conscious brain. But other people say they just "know." I have heard people say they received "a hit." It might be one word or a sentence. I have learned to ask Wisdom questions when I don't understand something. Yes, the questions are answered, usually before I finish asking the question. This may all sound way too "woo-woo" for you.

To that I will say, when you are ready to move into a place of willingness to connect with your Wisdom, or the Universe, or God, if that is your belief, you will connect. Your Spirit has been waiting for a lifetime (yours) to be invited to support and participate in your life.

Transforming your demons into your teachers

During the next year I sorted through every paper in the storage unit, sold the office furniture, dissolved the corporation and took many steps forward. The most important thing I did was to establish a new business – I began to serve as a Life Coach. This was work I longed to do, and now my opportunity began to open up.

Suddenly, I felt my life was "on purpose." I was doing what I really loved – helping others live their best lives. It was only then that I realized the demons, who created the uproar in my life, had actually created an opportunity for me to leave the work I had been doing to make room for me to grow into the person I am today. I had succeeded in transforming my demons into my teachers.

Without that experience, I might never have learned what I was really made of – or made for. With that knowledge, I was ready to move on in my life's journey. At first, I was simply putting one foot in front of the other, not exactly sure where the path was leading. Looking back now, I can see how my human plans were always dwarfed by my spirit's ideas. My spirit was always in the driver's seat, but often my fear tried to grab the wheel.

What life crisis could you look back on – from years ago or yesterday – when considered from a different point of view, might be seen as an opportunity? It might be an opportunity to simply understand what happened as a life lesson rather than as a disappointment or tragedy. It might open you up to forgiving and moving on. It might lead you to connecting to your own wisdom in understanding what the universe has in mind for you. Or maybe you will see a completely different reality than the one you have believed in for years.

Take a moment or two to reflect on the suggestions in the previous paragraph. Write down what comes to you. It doesn't have to make sense right now. Just write. If possible, bypass your brain and simply write what you feel. You might be surprised at what you find.

As we move on, I want you to keep in mind my stories are "Everywoman's" stories. They are filled with choices I made at certain crossroads and crises in my life. You make those choices, too. Along the way our paths are strewn with boulders and sharp turns and steep hills. Sometimes we experience smooth sailing. I'm inclined to share with you so you might ponder your own stories and imagine the inner-wisdom guiding you – even when it is not apparent and the journey is very difficult. We are never really alone. Let's take a step back together.

Part Two

Chapter 6

Being Intentional

Some days all we can manage to do is put one foot in front of the other. My experience has shown that if I just keep going slowly, or sometimes quickly, I will notice a shift and I am no longer trudging onward but moving joyously forward. Something will delight me, or put me in awe, or just make me smile. When that happens, I try to be intentional about noticing what it was. Taking in the moment. Delighting in life. That brings my focus back to what I want more of.

As a little girl of about three or four years old, my favorite place was face down in the cloth hammock in our backyard with the sun shining on me. If I put my face in just the right place I could see the grass through the fabric. I could watch the insects land on the grass or watch an earthworm crawl past. I don't know why that pleased me, but I felt like I was sneaking a peek at something that didn't know I was there. I loved the movement of the hammock, but I was so small that I couldn't easily make the hammock swing to and fro. If I reached my leg out as far as possible, I might be able to touch the ground long enough to push off and then I was in for a wonderful swing. The sun kissing my back, my face smushed into the fabric, my body swinging – I was in bliss. I loved it. I learned I could get to that place just as other children learn to get to places they enjoy. Children learn early to be intentional about getting what they want.

Why is it then, as adults, we forget to be intentional about seeking what we want and enjoy? Adults tend to take life very seriously. There are a lot of four-letter words we focus on, like work, and debt and loss and gain. I'll bet you have been there. I know I have. But when I remember to focus on the positive four letter words like goal or love or care, I can take that first step forward. It may be shaky, but it's a step in the right direction.

That is one important key to moving forward or moving on when hitting a bump in life. Focus on the positive possibility that you can create. When life throws me a sucker punch – like being told my husband wants a divorce, or the Civil Service position I thought was waiting for me in Seoul Korea has just been frozen by the President of the United States, I know my attitude is important and it is the only thing I can always count on. It is often the only thing we have control over. I believe I create my own reality by adjusting my attitude toward what life presents me.

At 21, I made a choice to join my soldier husband Bob in Seoul, Korea. I traveled as a U. S. Citizen, not a military dependent. Seoul was considered a hardship tour so wives and families of enlisted men were not expected to join their husbands. But by this time our marriage was fragile and I was adrift, still living in Missouri, far from my parents, grandmother and sister who were in Michigan. During the first 15 months of our marriage, we were together only five months, then separated for five, then together for the next five and separated again. The last five months of separation were the most difficult because I had almost no support system. When an opportunity arose for me to join my husband in Seoul, I had a very difficult time making a decision about going. I so wanted to join him, but I was worried about the bills my small income covered. What would happen if I couldn't find a job? We'd had to buy a mobile home in Missouri because there was nothing to rent. We had purchased a new car before we left for Missouri. There were school loans and utilities to pay. Even though I would be leaving, the bills would still need to be paid. My very responsible self struggled with the choice of staying put and keeping things as they were, or joining my husband and engaging in an adventure. However, an unexpected letter provided extra incentive for me to take the risk.

Bob was a chaplain's assistant and he had shared his concerns about our marriage and me with one of the chaplains he worked for. Father Healy wrote me a letter suggesting I join Bob in Seoul and experience things I would never forget. He told me I would never miss the money I would make if I stayed stateside. He was so wise and I am forever grateful to him for sharing his wisdom with a young woman he had never met. It was time for me to put one foot in front of the other.

In the hope of securing a Civil Service position at the 8th Army base in Seoul, I took a Civil Service exam and received my Clerk/Typist rating. I was assured a position would be available for me when I arrived in Seoul. After applying for a passport, I got my shots and saved enough money for my one-way ticket to Seoul. My in-laws agreed to keep our dog. I found a renter for our mobile home and stored the car with relatives. I knew the change I wanted and I discovered each step I needed to take to get to Seoul and back to Bob.

When I began, did I know all the steps to take for successful international travel? No. But after taking the first step, I knew the next question to ask and someone always supplied the answer. It was as if there were directional arrows pointing me on a forward path. Sometimes it was my mother on the phone, sometimes it was someone on the Army base. My father was busy trying to make sure my passport would arrive in time for my flight out of the country. Often, I found my own way. But people showed up just as I needed their help. I would be flying Detroit to Chicago, San Francisco, Honolulu, Tokyo and finally to Seoul.

A week before I was to leave, my passport had still not arrived. My father called the U.S. Passport Office in Chicago and found a helpful civil servant who took on the responsibility of making sure I could pick up my passport in his office in Chicago. This was tricky because I only had a two-hour window between the time my flight landed in Chicago and the next one left for San Francisco. In that two hours, I had to take a train and cab to the passport office, pick up my passport, walk a short distance to the Korean Embassy and get my visitor's visa stamp for Korea, then catch a cab back to the airport. I did it and made my flight. Whew! Deep breath with grateful thanks for all the people who made it possible. Even at 21, I knew I wasn't doing it all alone.

So far, so good. The next day I left San Francisco on a flight to Honolulu. When I checked into the airport in San Francisco I was told there was a cholera epidemic in Korea and I would need to get a cholera shot during my layover in Honolulu. I asked where to go and was directed to a clinic that would accept my military dependent medical coverage. Deep breath again.

I was getting closer to my destination. But it was not yet smooth sailing. While boarding the flight from Honolulu to Tokyo, I was told the ticket I booked was on an "illegal flight." Aghast at the idea I was involved in anything illegal, I asked what that meant. It turned out the amount of time required between international connecting flights was two hours and my ticket only allowed 1 hour and 40 minutes. We had severe headwinds and the flight was late. I missed my connecting flight to Seoul and spent the night in Tokyo. The airline covered the cost of the taxi, hotel room and dinner. Breathe again.

When I landed in Seoul the next day, my husband picked me up and during our tearful reunion he told me that President Johnson had frozen all government jobs as I was flying over the Pacific Ocean. There was no Civil Service job waiting for me. Timing is everything!

Here I was, my worst fears realized. No job. During my second week in Seoul, someone on the Army base told me, "You look very American. If you stand on a street corner in downtown Seoul someone will hire you to be their English tutor." Another person suggested I put a note on the bulletin board in the Republic of Korea Army (ROK) officers club saying I was an English tutor. I did, and later that evening I received a call from a ROK Army Lieutenant. He took me to the place where he was taking English classes and introduced me. I was now a Tutor of Spoken American English for a Korean school. Putting one foot in front of the other, I continued to BREATHE.

I quickly learned that our living conditions would be very different from anything I had ever experienced. During the next six months, my husband and I lived in Seoul in a Korean neighborhood. We shared a two-bedroom apartment with another young couple. The apartment even came with a maid. Miss Kim was in her late teens and a Korean War orphan. She had been hired by a tenant prior to our tenancy. Since she had no other home, she lived in the apartment and slept Korean style on the floor. She cleaned and did our laundry by hand. Miss Kim's story was only the first of many interesting things I learned about living in a different country. We needed her as much as she needed us. Without her we wouldn't have known how to pay our utility bills or how to find the man who brought the fuel we needed on a pushcart. We were living on the local economy. We bought groceries at the commissary and had access to the military PX for luxury goods. In many ways, we had the best of both worlds: the security of being connected to the American military; and the adventure of living in Seoul, Korea in 1969-70.

I had an even greater immersion in the culture because I built a clientele of students: some junior executives in the First National Bank of Seoul; a shipping entrepreneur who had made and lost three fortunes and spoke five languages but not English; the wife of the President of the Korean Aluminum Company who was a trained Social Worker; three sisters all named Mrs. Shin; and a variety of college students. What each of my students most wanted was to learn how to speak American English.

You might wonder how a young American could teach Korean students English. In Korea, all students studied Cambridge English in school from Junior High until they were no longer in school. But they all yearned to speak like Americans. Luckily, I found an American English textbook showing the lesson in English on the left page and Korean on the right page. The students could hear and see what I was teaching by reading the page in English, but referring to the Korean page if they didn't understand what I was asking. What a rich, rewarding experience I had over those six months! I loved my students and they seemed to love me back. I learned more from them than they from me, as is so often the case with teaching.

Each week my students would pay me in Korean Won. I would take the money to the post and exchange it for American dollars and deposit it in our checking account. The bills were being paid on time both in Korea and the United States. Over the seven months I lived there I had some students for the entire time. Others came and went as their schedules and finances allowed. Some students sent their drivers to bring me to their place of business or home. Sometimes I would take the bus to an agreed upon location. I had a few students who came to our apartment for class. I had a busy schedule and loved my work.

Bob's tour of duty and two-year draft would end in March. As Bob and I prepared to return to the states and civilian life, I found that after paying all of our bills we had exactly two dollars left. I gave him one and I kept one. He flew out five days before I was to leave. He would not be paid until he mustered out at Ft. Lewis, Washington. I made my dollar last all the way home! Now, when I say we had two dollars, I really mean that was all we had. No savings of any kind. Deep breath. During my seven months in Korea, I had made just enough money to pay our U.S. bills and with my husband's Army pay we had exactly enough for my one-way ticket back to Detroit, Michigan – plus our two dollars.

Father Healey was right. Going to live in Korea was a life-changing experience. I wouldn't have missed it for anything. Every one of the obstacles was surmountable. Every step led to the next step. I had created a reality that I couldn't have imagined. I created that reality by not being undone along the way.

The experience of my husband being drafted, in some ways, overwhelmed me. I was deeply depressed. When we could be together, I was happy. But each time change was thrown at me and I felt out of control, I lost my compass. I behaved in ways that did not fit my values. I allowed my attitude to become that of victim. I had not yet internalized the importance of being intentional. But at this point I was beginning to understand its importance.

While I was in Korea, I had found my center again through very intentional action. I could put one foot in front of the other to achieve the change I wanted. I wanted to be with my Bob and not be separated from him again. What I could not have imagined was the amazing story I would live during those six months in Korea. I was empowered by my small successes. My faith that all would be well grew. I had been able to pay all of our bills and still have two dollars left. I know it doesn't sound like a very high bar, but when you are only 21 years old and your whole life is changed with the delivery of your husband's draft notice, just living through those two years was a big deal.

If I had only known then that I had a wisdom coach with me all the time. All I needed to do was breathe in and ask for assistance. As a matter of fact, that wisdom was available and stepped in when needed. I just didn't have a full understanding that I could access that assistance whenever I needed it. I seemed to wait until things were frightening!

Now I ask you, what event in your life have you successfully made it through? If you can think of one right away, that is wonderful. Write it down. Remember the steps you took to achieve the outcome. This is the kind of exercise that helps remind your brain that you are perfectly competent.

Maybe you are in the middle of a very difficult time in your life. Do you know what outcome you would like? Do you have any idea what you might do or think to achieve that outcome in the future? Is there a step you could take that might improve the situation? Can you be intentional about moving forward just one step at a time? Is there someone to talk to, a choice to make, and information to gather? Breathe deeply, close your eyes, become very still, fill your abdomen and your diaphragm and your chest and then very slowly breathe out through your mouth. If that felt good, do it again. And, again. Be still and ask yourself what you most want to feel. Notice I am not asking you what you most want someone else to think or feel or do, because the only thing over which you have control is your attitude and your breath right now. Breathe in and invite your own Spirit to help you. You may immediately have a new idea, or you may "hear" an answer to your question. If nothing comes, be patient. This is a lot like learning anything new. It takes time to learn to listen for your Spirit to respond; and it is helpful to believe it is possible.

You might find it helpful to write about your thoughts. Or maybe you would rather spend some time in a meditative state clearing your mind to be open to a new thought or feeling. You have a very wise Spirit within. That spirit is connected to the wisdom of the Universe. But to get in touch with that part of yourself, you need to be quiet and calm and let that wise spirit speak. To hear, you must quiet your mind and your body. When words enter, listen carefully to them; if they are helpful it is most likely your introduction to your "Spirit."

Don't worry if you feel nothing on your first try or even your tenth try. It takes practice just like anything else worth doing does. So each time you feel yourself tense up or shut down, or act from a place of fear, take time to really breathe. Your body and your soul will be so grateful. It is like slaking a thirst with a long, cool drink of water. Refreshing!

Always remember to ask your Spirit for help. Your request can be as simple as breathing in deeply and pleading, "Spirit, please help me. What should I do?"

The practice of breathing is the next step. Let's see where it takes us.

Breathe

Chapter 7

Controlling Your Breath

Growing up, I remember I could get angry, but it wasn't my normal reaction to an argument. As I think back, I remember usually withdrawing a bit. When I say that, I don't mean I didn't stand my ground. Arguing never bothered me. But fighting was very uncomfortable for me. I'm not sure why. I just know that I never enjoyed fighting of any sort – certainly not physical fighting. I don't even like to watch combative sports like football or movies where there is physical or emotional fighting. Fighting with words to hurt someone felt horrible to me. The hard thing was I was good at it. I could win because I was quick and articulate. But if I said something hurtful, I felt remorse and guilt. If someone hurt me with cutting, critical words they seemed to stick. If possible, I would avoid anyone who was angry or mean.

Battle Mode

My sister Jane and I were attending the same small liberal arts college. She was a junior when I was a freshman. Our mother had often told us stories about her college experiences and her sorority sisters. It sounded glamorous and fun. She was, even then, active in her alumnae group. I suppose we both expected we would join sororities. Jane was a member of a sorority when I arrived on campus.

In the fall of my freshman year at college, I had a wonderful group of friends. We lived in the same dorm on the same floor along the same hall. I thoroughly enjoyed the camaraderie we had, eating together in the dining room most evenings, popping into one another's rooms to talk. Spring on campus meant sorority rush. Throughout my freshman year, I noticed the differences between the sororities and decided on the one I wanted to join.

Most of my freshman friends were planning to pledge the same sorority. It was so much fun to attend rush parties. But the morning that invitations were delivered under our doors, I didn't receive one. I was devastated. Everyone else in our group who wanted to pledge had received an invitation. Once again, I was left out. There was no one to have breakfast with, or lunch or dinner. Sorority pledges were required to eat with their sorority sisters. Suddenly all of my friends were very much, otherwise occupied.

For some people that might have been tolerable. But I have always valued my relationships with people above everything else. It would have been hard to imagine a more painful situation for me. If I had understood how important it is to breathe when in crisis, this would have been a saving grace. Instead, I cried and slept. I went to class, but then headed back to my room. Within the first 24 hours, one of the members of the sorority I had so hoped to join came to my room to see how I was. She had been assigned to me as a "Big Sister" when I first arrived on campus the previous fall. I have always been grateful to her for that visit. She told me she wasn't supposed to talk about the voting that took place, but she must have felt it was a quite a blow for me. She shared with me that only one girl voted no, which is called a blackball. I guess if you blackball someone you share your reason. I was told her reason was, "She (meaning me) has no right to try to join a sorority better than the one her sister belongs to." I love my sister, but we could hardly be more different from one another. She is a shy extrovert and happy to play a supportive role in most things. I enjoy being out in front. I had been elected to the student council the first week I was on campus. I loved to perform, both acting and dancing. I have never suffered from stage fright. I embrace leadership positions. I love working on a team.

Jane and her sorority sisters felt very badly for me. They said if they thought I wanted to join their sorority, they would have invited me. But theirs was not the sorority for me. It turned out, no sorority would be for me. Once again, Spirit knew what I needed for my life path. It took me years to understand that the pain of rejection for me would instill an important value that would play an important role in the rest of my life.

I needed to experience what it felt like to be completely rejected. That experience shaped my attitude toward exclusive organizations for the rest of my life. I have no interest in being a part of something where others are not welcome. The sad part was it took me many years - about 45 – to get past the way I learned the lesson. Part of the reason was the way it affected my self-image. I had suffered two similar losses during my senior year in high school. Both of those were created by adults who were in positions of power. Now my peers were rejecting me. I had no facility for understanding what I had done to deserve being excluded from things I really cared about. My way of dealing with it was to finish the year and transfer to a large state university.

The next fall, as a sophomore transfer student at Michigan State University, I began to find a community again, but it was difficult. I was no longer a freshman. There was no formal structure to meet other students from my class. Six weeks into my first term at Michigan State, just as I was beginning to find my place, I went home for the weekend. I came down with a serious sore throat. Eight days later, I was hospitalized with mononucleosis. Ten days later I went home to convalesce. I lost the entire term and was at a very low point. In December, before I returned to college, Bob and I became engaged. I returned to school and worked hard to complete my sophomore year. The following November we were married. At 19, I took on the adult responsibilities of marriage. Fifteen weeks after the wedding, Bob had been drafted, I was a young bride with a pile of bills trying to complete college classes and taking on two jobs to make ends meet. I was alone again.

Luckily, my parents and sister believed I was capable of doing almost anything I wanted to do. Their belief in me made it possible for me to keep putting one foot in front of the other. If I had known then what I know now about accessing my own Wisdom and the value of using breath to quiet and focus the mind, I feel certain my life would have been much easier. Instead I lived in "battle mode" for the next two years.

 I learned a lot over those first few years of our marriage. Just as I was learning to be a wife, Bob was drafted and I was alone. Then we were together and I began to be a wife again. In a short while, he was in Korea: I was alone again; I learned how to survive in some difficult circumstances. I learned to live overseas and was finally able to be a wife living with her husband. Several years later, I learned to be a mother. Then I learned to be a divorced, single mother. In fact, I learned a lot over the next 20 years! One thing I depended on was that there was more than just me. Something more. At the time I called it God. Now I call it Spirit. I will always have more to learn.

When I met my wonderful husband Michael, I was still experiencing a lot of turmoil. In fact meeting Michael led to my being sexually harassed by my boss at work. He knew I had been divorced and believed that when I was ready to be in a relationship it would be with him. I had no interest in him at all. When he learned I was seriously dating someone, he told me I would have to leave my job. This was 1986 in a Fortune 50 company! In the 1980s, it was dangerous for a Fortune 50 company to be sued for sexual harassment because large monetary penalties were being handed down. Luckily for me, management was on the lookout for such things and my manager must have looked like a typical suspect. I was asked point-blank to tell someone very high up in the corporation the truth about why I was leaving my current position. With great hesitation, I did tell the truth. It turned out my experience was the least offensive many women he had worked with had experienced. After further investigation, he was escorted from his office and fired. I felt some of the things rape victims feel - embarrassment, questioning what I did to lead to his thoughts and guilt that he lost his job. I knew consciously I had done nothing wrong and neither had the four other women whose stories were worse than mine. But the culture of my generation taught women that we were always the responsible party. Again, I felt like I had been through a battle. But this time I had a weapon that protected me in both body and spirit.

Coming home to Michael's loving embrace filled my heart to overflowing. He demanded nothing and freely offered everything I needed. We were married six months after my boss was fired. This time real joy followed the battle! After almost 30 years of marriage to Michael, I still feel so grateful to love and be loved by him. Sometimes two souls fit together perfectly. One of the greatest gifts of my human existence is the love we share. Ours is truly a marriage of equals. Although it took a few years to rid myself of the discomfort of my encounter with sexual harassment, I was made stronger through the experience.

Through all the ups and downs, I kept breathing! But it was the kind of breathing we need to stay alive. I didn't have any idea about the influence that breath had on my body, mind and spirit. It wasn't hard to learn once I was introduced to the idea. In fact controlling your breath comes quite naturally. When we sit still in a resting state our breathing tends to be quite shallow. We are not usually aware of our breathing. When you actually think about your breath, it seems as if you haven't really been breathing at all. When you experience that feeling you will most likely feel drawn to breathe in deeply.

Breathing
Until I connected with the beautiful souls who populate the spiritual entrepreneur community, I often found myself in battle mode. Once I was introduced to a smattering of Zen, a

touch of Yoga and Hindu wisdom, the Tao and most especially the practice of breathing, my life began to shift into ease.

When exercising you begin to breathe more deeply and more quickly. Running, swimming or any active sport requires that we control our breathing for greatest efficiency. When you are in an emotionally charged state it can be difficult to "catch your breath." Being able to regulate your breathing is step one in learning to use your breath to connect to your inner wisdom.

Your physical body needs to process oxygen through your heart and lungs to keep functioning properly. That process of breathing not only affects your body, it also affects your brain and your mind. I think of our bodies as the wild, primal part of us. When I speak of the brain, I am referring to the physical organ in the body. When I speak of the mind, I am referring to that place where thoughts, beliefs and memories are created. Your brain is the mechanism that provides storage and allows access to higher-level thinking. Just as your heart and lungs help you process oxygen, they are not the oxygen. Oxygen is breathed in from our atmosphere, but our respiratory system makes it accessible for our body's use. Likewise your brain is not your mind, but it is the organ that allows your mind to develop and function.

Our breath, when used correctly, has the ability to calm our bodies, just as lowering your head quiets the body and closing your eyes calms the mind. Your breath connects you to Spirit or Wisdom. It allows you to think beyond your physical reality. Breathing deeply and calmly sends your brain the message, "all is well and safe." It provides a pathway beyond all you can see, hear, touch, taste, and smell. Your breath opens a point of access to the place where creativity begins. It is where we turn when trying to solve puzzles, find the right words, answer questions, seek understanding, and learn.

That said, how can our breath lead us to our wisdom? Earlier I mentioned how we tell children and adults to "breathe" when they are upset. We begin by finding a stillness within through meditation or simply breathing slowly and deeply. This slow intake of breath allows you to access the answers we all have within ourselves. Some people believe they access the wisdom of the Universe or Source. Others believe they access the wisdom of their Creator. My experience is, it doesn't matter what belief you embrace. What does matter is believing it is possible to connect to wisdom that is inexplicable, wisdom that offers you answers that can direct you to your own fulfillment. You are here to live into the human condition and all of its beautiful, exciting, sensory experiences. You came into this life fully equipped to live your best life. You came with everything you need. It is up to you to discover how to access all of your resources.

My first awareness of accessing something more than my physical self, my own knowledge and life experience, was when I was asked to speak at certain church functions. Sometimes I would work very hard to prepare just the right words. But when I spoke, the words on the page paled in comparison to the thoughts and words that came out. I didn't know I was going to say them. I didn't know where the thoughts came from that emerged from my lips extemporaneously. Those words had more immediate meaning for the congregation than my prepared thoughts. After several years of having this happen, I fell upon the notion that it might be a good idea to ask for inspiration from the Divine when I knew I would be asked to share my thoughts. That was the dawning of my understanding that something much bigger than just good old Susan was doing the talking. I had to let go of my proud ego and acknowledge the wisdom was from deep within, but not from my personal human experience. I didn't understand where it came from exactly; but I knew I could trust it to be there, if I remembered to ask.

Slowly I realized I could ask for guidance when seeking the right words or advice. But only recently did it occur to me that I might start each day with a request for access to this wisdom. Sometimes I still forget. I did say this was a practice and I imagine the 10,000-hour rule applies here as well.

Do you know the 10,000-hour rule? It is that, to master anything, we must practice it for 10,000 hours. The good news is that during the accumulation of the 10,000 hours, we will improve even if we haven't mastered the subject yet. So I don't despair, I simply practice, every time I remember!

As years pass, I learn to depend on the Wisdom that resides within. We all have it. The challenge is to trust that we have it, practice using it and make it a part of our everyday experience. At this point you may be asking, "How do I get started? How can I trust that the right words will be there for me? How will I know if it is only my own thoughts or words of Wisdom?" My answer is, with practice you will KNOW that what you are sharing is right by the way you feel about the message. It will flow out of you. It is not hard work. It will feel right. Sometimes you will be delivering what people want to hear. Sometimes you will be unpopular with what you have to share. But you will feel at ease within. Your messages will be filled with your own experience, enlightened by Wisdom.

Before I speak, in meetings or from the stage, in one-to-one conversations or to groups, I take a moment to close my eyes, bow my head and take a couple of deep, slow in-breaths and let each one out slowly, all the while asking for wisdom to find the right words and share what is best for the universe. I don't make a show of my preparation. Sometimes I do it well before I arrive. When I find myself in an unexpected situation and I know I must tap into my wisdom, I can follow my breathing protocol and no one even notices. But sometimes I forget and that is when I get into trouble. My ego takes over and cuts off inner-wisdom. That can be a recipe for disaster.

Daily practice helps keep me in touch with the whole idea of accessing inner wisdom. I use it for every step of my life ... when I remember! I use it when I am gardening, or grocery shopping, or finding which way to go when confused about directions. But when I get busy and forget to seek wisdom, I find myself out of sync. Sometimes I forget to acknowledge the wisdom within. That's when I know it's time to quiet my mind. When under stress I can forget for days or weeks at a time that the wisdom is not mine, it is a "shared resource." When that happens and I catch myself, I begin the practice of mindful breathing and seeking the advice of the Wisdom within. It certainly takes more time to reach the best solution or find the right words when I have taken over with my own ideas instead of accessing my wiser thoughts from within. It is important to practice mindfulness.

To me, mindfulness is being consciously aware of my words and actions – understanding the wide reach and repercussions my words can have. Mindfulness causes me to be reflective about the way in which I interact with all living things. It draws me up short when I am cut off in traffic and I become irritated. Mindfulness calls me to breathe deeply and remind myself that I have no idea what just happened for the other person.

I will never forget the early evening over a decade ago when my husband and I were following our daughter and son-in-law with our infant grandson in their new car. We were stopped at a stoplight behind their car. The light turned green, they pulled into the intersection and right before our eyes a car ran the red light and crashed into the driver's side of their car. I screamed and threw open the door to our car. As I raced to their car, I yelled, "Are you okay? Is anyone hurt?" I couldn't get to my grandson's infant carrier fast enough to make sure he was okay. He didn't even start to cry until he heard me screaming. That is a grand example of me not being mindful. I was shaking all over and I remember my son-in-law wrapping his arms around me asking me if I was all right. Talk about someone able to access his own Wisdom! After all the assessments were completed, no one in their car was seriously injured.

I was so angry with the woman who hit their car that I went over to her car and berated her for not paying attention. I regret that action to this day. I have no idea what caused her to not be paying attention, but she had two children in her car. I would like to think that today I would react more mindfully. I might still be shocked and frightened until I knew everyone was all right. I hope I would not yell at anyone. I am not proud of this example, but it is my truth and I always have a lot more to learn.

Using breath to calm my wild, untamed human body is a practice. That means if we consciously use this technique, we can create a habit. The same is true for mindfulness. Reading about it here will not create a habit. Practicing it many times a day will create the habit. Once the habit is formed it can become a natural part of your life. When it is a part of your life, you will find yourself in the middle of a deep, mindful breath when stress hits or you are seeking to tap into your own internal wisdom.

My friends and family, clients, even strangers are sometimes surprised to hear me interrupt them with the words, "I am going to ask you to take a deep, slow, breath, and hold it, then breathe out slowly." I do this when I sense that their thinking is controlled by fear and ego in a way that prevents them from accessing a "place of possibility." Sometimes they do, sometimes they don't. I breathe with them. It is amazing what can shift with one or two breaths. On occasion people are irritated, embarrassed or feel that I am demeaning them by asking them to breathe. I understand, as there was a time I would have felt the same way. If only we were given that instruction manual on the day we began to breathe. Instead we must each discover it for ourselves or with the help of friends or practitioners.

If you have trouble remembering to practice, put little reminders around your home and work spaces. It could be a small marble or stone. It could be a picture of something that represents peace and tranquility to you. It could be just the word BREATHE written on a sticky note. Once you give the object the task of reminding you to breathe mindfully, it will do its job!

Most of this chapter has been about words, but there are many times we might need to access our Wisdom for actions. I will never forget a visiting minister who spoke about her mother telling her, "Nothing is lost that can't be found." She explained that she thought she had lost something that was very important. Remembering what her mother said she repeated over and over, nothing is lost that can't be found. Later that day she found what she was looking for. That one sentence opened up a possibility mindset for a lifetime for me. At the time I thought, "If I just repeat this when I lose something I will find it." Sure enough, it worked. Because I had no experience where this kind of thinking was concerned, I thought it was limited to finding "things." But over the years I have come to realize it is the perfect invitation for Spirit to guide me. Remember, I said we come equipped with everything we need. In my case, I believe if I ask Spirit for help, I will receive whatever wisdom is needed.

Please understand this doesn't mean I get everything I ask for. Sometimes the answer is, "No," or "Not now."

If you believe all wisdom comes from your brain, that's fine too. But Spirit's gifts of wisdom are often far beyond anything I could know from my own life experiences. So when I lost my great-grandmother's earring in the snow in the parking lot behind my office, I repeated, "Nothing is lost that can't be found." I didn't find it, not then anyway. But I do have plenty of patience. So each day I would look, repeating the words. Two months later, after the winter snow had melted, after hundreds of cars had driven through the parking lot, pulling into and out of parking spots, I looked down at the crumbling blacktop and saw a little gold earring. There it was, a small gold hoop earring, well over 100 years old, undamaged, fully functioning and found! Nothing is lost that can't be found. I can't ever prove that it was there the whole time. I can't prove my mantra allowed me to find it. But I can't prove it didn't either. This story is not about facts, although it is factual. It is about belief and trust in something more. It is about accepting that even when we don't know how or why or what the answers to our questions are, we can ask and know that an answer will come to us. But we have to ask and be patient while waiting for the answer. It is important to believe an answer will come.

Now when I misplace something I easily remember to repeat, "Nothing is lost that can't be found." I save a lot of time because I am focusing on what I want, not bemoaning what I've lost. Even when the backing from my new diamond earring dropped out of my hand, rolled off the dresser, and hit the hardwood floor and I couldn't find it anywhere, I said, "Nothing is lost that can't be found." I moved the furniture. I went through the box next to the dresser. No sign of it. I cleaned under the bed and still nothing. We moved 90 miles.

With everything removed from our bedroom, still no sign of the backing

One day, last year, I decided to clean out my sewing basket. I rewound spools of thread, organized the needles, pins, scissors, snaps, hooks and eyes. When I reached the bottom of the basket, there it was! The backing to the earring I had dropped two years before had taken up residence in the bottom of the sewing basket, which had been tightly closed with the lid in place when the backing fell. How it got in there I do not know. But I do know it wasn't lost – it was found. Once again I had focused on what I wanted – to find that backing.

I was once given a small sticker that had a black dot on it with the instructions to place it somewhere I would see it when I rose in the morning. I decided the best place would be on the toilet paper holder in our bathroom! Its purpose was to remind me to be optimistic. That was more than 25 years ago; the dot is still there and I am still reminded to be optimistic. It makes me smile each time I see it, a little black dot with a lot of staying power. Even on my worst days, I still see it and know what I am supposed to do. Pick whatever item will work for you and remember that all of this is a practice. Like playing the piano, if you don't practice, you won't be able to play well. That is a good metaphor for life.

So along with whatever practices are already a part of your life, I suggest you add remembering to BREATHE when life throws you a curve. But as with the simple suggestions above you will need to practice regularly to develop the habit of breathing to create a calm space within yourself. That will allow you to find your own place of possibility.

The next chapter will offer suggestions and practical guidance to connect to your own Wisdom. Before you move on, let's try a few of those deep, cleansing breaths. It is helpful to simply be. If you find it is difficult to think of nothing, go ahead and in your mind ask a question about anything you would like help with. Then while breathing sit quietly. Words may "float" into your mind.* Pay attention. Those words may well be your connection to wisdom. With some practice you will begin to know the difference between your random thoughts, your conscious thoughts and wisdom.

The first time I tried this, I was looking for something that was just gone. I had looked in every imaginable place. In desperation I stopped, breathed in and out three or four times and asked, "Okay Spirit, I can't find that paper. Please lead me to it." I then opened my eyes, walked directly to a drawer, opened it and under several layers of papers there was the sheet I was looking for. Simple as that.

For a long time, I thought that was interesting. After I made a few more connections on a much deeper level, I began to understand there is a resource within that I can access. That was more than 10 years ago. It took me a long time to connect the dots, but I was on my way to discovering how to Breathe into Wisdom.

* Some people report the voice they hear sounds like their own. Others say it doesn't sound like anyone they know. Still others report there is no voice. They simply know what the answer is. However your Spirit responds is right!

Breathe

Chapter 8

Breathe into Wisdom

In this chapter, I'd like you to meet your breath. Get to know it and become familiar with your wonderful ability to clear your mind and simply concentrate on your ability to participate in that beautiful, life-sustaining experience of breathing.

1. **Begin with a mind open to possibility.**
2. **Close your eyes.**
3. **Bow your head.**
4. **Breathe in slowly and deeply, filling your chest and abdominal cavity.**
5. **Hold that breath for a couple of seconds.**
6. **Release your breath slowly through your mouth through your pursed lips.**

7. **Pause for a few seconds.**
8. **Continue to breathe, simply focusing on your in-breath slowing feeling the breath fill your belly and lungs until they are full. Then hold it for a moment longer. Then very slowly breathe out until you find yourself pushing out the last bit of breath. Wait a moment and begin again.**

Continue with your in-breath, hold, out-breath, hold, in-breath and so on for ten rounds.

This type of breathing will calm your brain and encourage relaxation of your body. I find it is a wonderful tool that allows me to redirect my thoughts. When I am anxious, a few rounds of breathing allow me to become grounded and better able to think more clearly. I can focus. This way of breathing is a practice. It took me some time to stop worrying if I was doing it right. It took even more sessions to begin to feel the benefit. Some people fall easily into this practice; for others it may take several sessions. Don't worry, everyone gets there. But, as with any change or transition, your intention sets the stage.

Once you are comfortable with the breathing practice described above, I invite you to simply focus on an experience or feeling that seems to be occupying your thoughts. It might be a mistake you feel you have made, or an upsetting exchange with someone. It could be a question for which you are seeking an answer. You might be seeking guidance on the next step to take, or which words to say in a certain situation. This is all about you and what you would like to explore. It's your turn to breathe into your own wisdom.

Breathing to Connect to Source

When I refer to Source, I am referring to that which supplies all that we need physically, mentally, spiritually, and emotionally. It is the source of your Wisdom.

You might be more comfortable using the term God, Allah, the Tao, or the I Am. Whatever name works best for you is the one you should use. This is not meant to be religious in any way. It is meant to be a totally inclusive practice, available to anyone, anywhere, at any time. It requires no equipment, no belief, only your intention. There is no room in this practice for self-criticism, only love.

When you are ready to connect to your source of strength and wisdom:
1. **Begin with a few breathing rounds.**
2. **After the first three or four deep breaths, greet your Spirit using whatever name you choose.**
3. **Ask to learn whatever will be in your highest and best good.**
4. **Let your mind make a simple statement or ask a simple question about your issue or concern.**

5. Let your thought be a simple, nonjudgmental statement.

6. Continue to breathe in and out slowly and deeply.

7. Sometimes you may experience a thought that offers direction or an actual solution.

8. Sometimes nothing will come. That's fine. If you are willing to continue with breathing and allow your mind to simply clear, there can be great benefit.

9. At times you may find just when you think you are not accessing anything but empty thoughts – the answer will come through "loud and clear."

10. Sometimes you will simply be immediately calmer. Later in the day or night the answer you seek will appear.

11. Trust what comes, when it comes, as being in your highest and best good.

This process takes patience and practice. Be ready to accept that an answer will not necessarily arrive in your perfect time frame. You may discover you are not asking the right question. Your expectations may be screaming, while your wisdom whispers.

After I had closed my business and continued to struggle with feelings of victimization I focused my thoughts on proving to others that I had done a good job. I asked myself over and over how could I prove how unjust and unfortunate the previous 18 months had been. Suddenly, in one moment, I discovered I had been asking the wrong question for two years! Instead of asking, "How can I make them see they are wrong?" I thought of more constructive, more purposeful questions to ask. The questions were, "Why did this happen? What am I supposed to learn?" I asked once and the Universe immediately provided an answer to the question. It took almost no time for me to "get it." My mind was clear; I had to let go of the baggage of concern I had been carrying. Immediately there was space for joy and I welcomed it. Something triggered the issue I had tried to address for two years. After changing the question, I realized I could enjoy the benefit of a divine answer to the question as it should have been asked! Let that be a lesson to me ... and you.

Having received the answer, it was time to simply let it go with a request that the Universe/Source/Wisdom provide that which was in my highest and best good.

The sticky wicket with this sort of practice is we must willingly accept that we don't always know what is in our highest and best good. At times like this, thinking back to the loss of my long-term client or my first marriage, the practice feels hard. I didn't want either of those losses to happen. But happen they did. To find a new love that led to a truly happy, joy-filled marriage, I had to move on. To retire from a way of work that had run its course and begin to live my life "on purpose," I had to give up the old work to make room for the new. Had I recognized that at the time, I might have been more accepting. Or maybe my stubborn, human self was just not in a place to find ease with the process of losing that which I believed I needed. I just wasn't coming from a place of trusting anyone or anything, but my conscious self.

If I had been able to ask the question, "Is there something better to come?" or "Will I be okay even if this awful thing happens?" I might have found more solace. I was asking the question, "How can I make them see they are wrong?" The wrong questions lead us down a dead–end path. Luckily, the Universe knows not to answer such questions.

The first question that comes to mind might be, "Why?" followed by "How can I take another breath with this loss?" As grief subsides, the next question one might ask is, "How can I use this experience for my highest and best good?" I wasn't raised to ask questions like that. That was certainly not my first reaction to shocking news or loss. But when we reach that place where we are alone and in despair, after the anger and rage and grief subside, the wisdom within waits for that very question. It is the question filled with life-affirming hope in the midst of despair. Hope is the first step back from the precipice. Take a deep, healing breath and breathe into the Wisdom of hope.

Breathing into Hope

As I stood at the bottom of the basement stairs, still in my pajamas at two o'clock in the afternoon, I heard the door close. My husband had taken the last thing he wanted from the house and moved out. My despair was beyond belief. How could this have happened? What was left? The man I loved deeply, no longer loved me. I could barely breathe. But I did take that next breath, and the next and the next. Hope is that fragment we cling to when we feel everything else has been torn from us.

Somewhere deep within, pulsing beneath the surface, my spirit kept communicating with my physical body. My spirit encouraged me. Days passed. I dressed. I went to work. I took care of my daughter. Months passed and I continued to fulfill my responsibilities. That is the first step we can take when we feel loss, pain, devastation. We behave responsibly. It is in our core to take care of our children, to feed, shelter and clothe them, and, by extension, ourselves. We do what needs to be done.

This doesn't mean you don't also feel rage and despair at times. The feelings of rage begin to abate very slowly and you feel a glimmer of hope. You keep on going. As the months pass you will begin to feel real hope. You will notice you have something to look forward to. You will find yourself chuckling for the first time. You will notice a warmth inside that feels foreign, because it has been missing from your life since your loss. But your Spirit has not lost any of its ability to move you forward in your life. Your emotional body may have lost its way for a while, but your Spirit never forgets your true life path.

So much was lost during the Great Recession, which began in 2008: jobs, careers, homes, retirement funds, pensions. The safety nets of our lives were casualties of the economic downturn. During this time many people lost faith in the American Dream. Some people are still suffering from those losses and may never recover financially. Others have recovered and are moving into their new realities. Hope plays a big part in allowing people to accept the losses and begin again, sometimes with new priorities and new possibilities.

Hope may not be a strategy, but it is an attitude that can lead to a new way of being. That kind of attitude is everything when it comes to recovering from anything. Medical research shows attitude plays a large role in patient recovery after surgery or illness. Hope helps us focus on the future. Focusing on the future allows us to begin to create our new reality. Hope allows us to live into that reality.

Breathing into hope literally means inhaling slowly and deeply. Fill your belly and lungs with a slow, deep breath and hold it for a few seconds. Then slowly exhale through your mouth. Close your eyes and bow your head while you practice this breathing. Pause for a moment while focusing on your question to the Universe/God/Allah/Source/Wisdom. Ask how you might begin to achieve the best possible outcome for yourself and the world. Repeat breathing, slowly and deeply. Envision yourself right in the middle of achieving that outcome. Really see yourself rejoicing and reveling in all that you imagine is possible. Remember this is a practice. Remember the 10,000 hours one must spend practicing to become a master of anything? The good news is that while we work toward mastery of breathing, if we choose that goal, we will enjoy the benefits of learning a little more every time we practice.

You might enjoy practicing this breathing exercise several times a day when you feel overwhelmed with loss. It may seem difficult to imagine you could do this, but try it. Your spirit will be fed and your brain will develop new neural pathways. Recent scientific research dedicated to understanding the plasticity of the brain proves this. Take the example of Jill Bolte Taylor. At 37, this Harvard trained brain scientist suffered a stroke that damaged the left side of her brain. In her book, *My Stroke of Insight*, she explains what the experience of having a stroke felt like, her recovery from the subsequent surgery, and how she ultimately regained everything she had lost and more.

One of the most interesting insights from the book is how Taylor was able to change parts of her personality by focusing on the behaviors she wanted to adopt and ignoring old patterns she wished to eliminate. She says, "As biological creatures, we are profoundly powerful people. Because our neural networks are made up of neurons communicating with other neurons in circuits, their behavior becomes quite predictable. The more attention we pay to any particular circuit, or the more time we spend thinking specific thoughts, the more impetus those circuits or thought patterns have to run again with minimal external stimulation."[14]

She adds, "We are designed to focus in on whatever we are looking for. If I seek red in the world, I will find red everywhere."[15]

If you are looking for hope, you will find it. Does that mean you will always get what you want? Probably not. With practice and focus, you will find a way to deal positively with what comes your way.

Your breath allows you to access your inner wisdom. Your brain allows you to reprogram your thinking. Remember, we focus on whatever we are looking for.

Breathing into Yourself

Full-term, healthy baby bodies come into this world with an ability to breathe. They don't have to think about it; they just breathe. In an effort to calm toddlers and children who are crying and very upset we often tell the child, "Take a deep breath." This speaks not to the body as much as the mind. Humans instinctively know that taking a deep breath calms us. Unfortunately, we don't always remember to apply this wisdom to our own lives.

Most teenagers have angst-filled moments. I had a few of my own. How we deal with those moments can be milestones in our development. I was selected to represent my church's youth fellowship in the Detroit Youth Presbytery, a collection of the 101 Presbyterian churches in the greater Detroit area in 1963. I was elected secretary that year and wanted to run as vice-moderator the next year. The advisor said I would not be allowed to. I wasn't sure why, so I asked and was told that was just the way it would be. My friends told me they had a plan. The evening of the election they nominated me from the floor and I won the election. I never knew why the adult advisor tried to prevent me from running, but I he didn't stop me from serving once I was elected.

My high school years were filled with opportunities to learn about being a leader. I liked taking responsibility for creating successful outcomes. Although at that time I wouldn't have been able to describe my enjoyment that way. I enjoyed performing in school plays, serving as President of the Drama Club, and actively participating as chairperson of several committees in our youth fellowship at church. I enjoyed the challenges of working with others to create meaningful events while having fun.

Having paid my dues by serving on committees from seventh grade through high school, I set my sights on being the moderator of the Senior High Youth Fellowship at my local church. I learned from one of the church staff that the opportunity to stand for election would not be given to me by the adult who was the youth fellowship advisor.

I had run for student council almost every year in high school and lost. I never gave up. I wasn't devastated by not winning. It was not being allowed the opportunity to be selected or rejected by my peers that seemed unfair. I never understood what the advisor's motivation was, but my best friend was given the coveted position and another friend was given the vice-moderator position. Disappointed and hurt, I was placed in yet another committee position and faithfully fulfilled the duties. It felt like applying for the college you have dreamed of attending and learning that your transcript was never reviewed before the decision was made to send you a rejection letter.

That was a life-changing moment for me. I didn't know it at the time. I only felt hurt. If I had known then what I know now, I might have understood that the whole loss was not necessarily about me not getting something, but someone else needing it more. I won't ever know how that knowledge coupled with the two experiences I have highlighted here might have changed my life. Instead, I moved forward determined to not let a rejection like that happen again without at least finding out why.

I believe that if we miss a life lesson when it is presented the first time, or the second, it will be presented repeatedly with the same opportunity until we learn the lesson. The same kind of thing happened again the very next year. Again, the pain and disappointment brought me to my knees. I didn't understand what I was doing to deserve such a thing AGAIN! Even more determined to move forward, I began to really be on guard against unfairness, not only for myself, but for others as well. Both times I removed myself from the "painful sphere." Each time I began again, more determined to not let that happen again!

From the outside, my strategy for coping with the pain and disappointment seemed to work. It looked like I recovered fairly well from the experiences and moved forward in my life. But the fact was I wasn't working through the loss, I was escaping from the loss. Until I learned the lessons the experiences held for me, and really understood my reactions to them, I wasn't moving forward. I was simply moving around.

Over the years there were hints that I was unable, or unwilling to decode. One friend said, "You know your reactions in life are simply reflections of yourself." But I didn't really understand what that meant. When reading, I often came across books and articles delivering the same message. Over the years, I learned more about myself. I was able to intuitively understand what was not being said as clearly as I understood the words of a conversation. I was successful in school, business and life.

Despite the minor losses in high school, the somewhat greater personal loss in college and a heartbreaking divorce, I still felt all I could do was react. But it wasn't until I was dealt yet one more blow to my ego that I finally began to understand what all those messengers were trying to tell me. So I will try to deliver my understanding of my life lesson as succinctly as possible. These are my ten commandments:

1. *The only person over whom you have control is yourself — you can't change other people.*
2. *You won't always get what you want.*
3. *Not getting what you want won't kill you.*
4. *Search for an understanding of why you wanted "it" so very much.*
5. *Imagine what will be allowed to open up in your life because the loss has made room for something else to come into your life.*
6. *Understand that your reaction to the loss is you creating your reality.*
7. *Forgive whatever or whoever you believed caused your disappointment and hurt, even when it is you who needs the forgiveness.*
8. *Remember you can access all the answers to your life's questions but you must ask for them.*
9. *Be patient with yourself. Take time to feel what you need to feel and think what you need to think.*

10. *Love yourself so much that you feel safe enough to discover your own truth about the reality you create.*

How do those ten points work in reality? It has to do with understanding that only you have the answers to your life's big questions. In other words, you don't need anyone else to provide the answers. That is not to say you don't need other people, friends, family, or a good education or a coach or counselor every now and then. You may need and enjoy great benefit from any or all of these. Humans are not meant to live in a vacuum. We are communal beings. Basically, we come with wisdom that is available to us at all times.

The trick is learning and remembering to access that wisdom. That brings us to the purpose of this book. To access your own personal font of wisdom you must breathe. At this point you are either with me or you are thinking, "Yah, right!" You may be saying to yourself, my father died when I was 10, or my husband left me to raise our children alone, or I watched my child die right in front of me while I could do nothing to help, or I just lost my job, my house, my spouse, my family. The list can go on and on. I do understand that helpless feeling. The one where you are not sure you can even take another breath. You don't know how you will live. I've been there. Not with your particular challenges and life experiences, but with my own. Each time we experience a loss, we must make up our minds to keep breathing into our own Wisdom.

Sometimes it takes courage, other times we simply enjoy a lack of fear. Either way, we need to find our own answers. Breathing deeply into your own inner wisdom is a tool that is readily available.

Here are some simple instructions to begin your breathing exercise:

1. Sit comfortably and begin by closing your eyes and bowing your head.
2. Slowly breathe in through your nose. Feel the breath pass through your nostrils.
3. Feel your lungs and abdomen inflate slowly. Really concentrate on that intake of breath.
4. Hold it for a couple of seconds longer than is natural for you.
5. Then begin a slow and steady exhale through your mouth. You may either purse your lips and blow out slowly or open your mouth and let your breath out with an "Ahhhhh."
6. Be acutely aware of how your breath feels, how your whole body feels.
7. Do this three times, slowly and with careful attention to your breath.

If your mind wanders from your breath, simply bring your attention back to your breathing. This is a step to help you become present in your body.

Now you will connect body and mind by focusing on the problem or questions you wish to address. Think about the most concise, honest way you can ask your question. Take your time with your eyes closed and head bowed. Continue with your gentle, steady inhalations and exhalations as you pose your question in your mind. Focus your mind on your question and your body on your breathing. Be easy with yourself. Let your mind play with the question a little, let it tumble around in there. Change the words as little or as much as you need, until you feel you have the specific question you want to address. Allow your thoughts to flow in and through you. You will know when you have come upon an important kernel.

If nothing feels quite right, try to rephrase the question. You might ask, "How might this actually help me?" or "What might I learn from ...?" In other words, shift your perspective a bit to open possibility. If you are stuck with a preconceived notion of what the answer is, you might try, "Even though I know (fill in your preconceived answer), how else might I think about this?"

You might even ask yourself, "What frightens me the most about (state the question, issue or situation)?" If it feels right, follow that thread while continuing to breathe in deeply and completely and exhaling through your mouth.

Your breath affects your body. In fact, it connects your body and mind to your essence or your Spirit. Your Spirit connects to your source of wisdom. Your ability to connect came into the world with you and develops over your lifetime with practice and attention. Your ability to connect will wither if you don't use it. If you choose to connect to Wisdom it will be only a breath away.

There is one more piece of the puzzle where the mind/body connection occurs. It is something we are all familiar with. Our ego, or what I like to call our "monkey brain," is that part of us that is constantly reminding us of our shortcomings, our failures and what we must fear to protect ourselves. It often tells you, "Be careful, you did that before and failed, or you were hurt," or … or … or. The list is an endless litany of every bad thing that might happen. It is that voice in your head telling you, "Be careful." For some of us it is the voice that reminds us to think small by saying, "You can't do this," or "You don't deserve that."

In truth, it is there to protect you but it is an overprotective, very primitive safety system. To reach beyond your comfort zone is to grow and experience more of life. It is that moment when you face your ego and say, "Thank you. I will be careful, but I am going to try this because I believe it will be a good experience. It is what I want to do with my life." Your ego is a part of you and deserves to be respected, just as your physical and spiritual bodies do. But be mindful when it's overprotective.

At this point, your mind is engaged with the issue you are addressing, your body is involved with your breathing, your spirit is open to providing you with answers from your source of wisdom. This may all be new to you, and if it is, just relax and try to suspend your disbelief. Imagine this is like your first plane ride. You trusted the pilot to get the plane up in the air safely, flying to your destination and landing without mishap. You didn't really understand how it all worked, but you landed safely without understanding all the details.

Spend as long as you wish in this state, breathing in and out slowly. At first you may only want to spend three to five minutes. This is a practice and it takes time to learn to be comfortable simply sitting quietly, breathing and focusing your thoughts on one issue. Your mind may wander in another direction and you may want to explore that thought, or you may discover it is trying to avoid thinking about the issue. If that happens, gently invite your mind to move back to your intended focus.

You may be very experienced in meditation and find it is easy to be still and focused. If this is the case, you are ready to dig deeply into your thoughts. As they arise, test them to determine where they will take you next. If you end up feeling emotions that are uncomfortable, explore what makes them uncomfortable. If tears come, let them come. If laughter comes, let it roll, but do not stop focusing on your chosen issue. You are on your way to breathing into your inner wisdom!

I have found that I can usually make a useful discovery that will be a kernel of an idea. I will think about it for a few hours or a few days before I return to the issue. Some people refer to this as "peeling the onion." If your issue has been with you for quite a while it may take a few sessions to dig deeply enough to get to the real wisdom – the life lesson you will learn and use from this time forward.

Each time you discover a new life lesson, it will jostle around until it finds its place in your entire life landscape. From now on that lesson will be added to your own library of life lessons and will become another tool available to you as you continue to gain perspective.

Breathe

Chapter 9

Gaining Perspective

One of the most obvious, and at the same time most profound, things I've learned is that perspective is developed over time – a long time. Distance brings things into focus. When we have an experience, we believe we understand what is happening in the moment. On the surface that is true. But with time, we develop a perspective of how that moment fits into our whole life experience. Its meaning in our lives may not be fully revealed for years.

Sharing a couple of personal examples might be helpful here. The first one has to do with my first husband choosing to ask for a divorce. It took more than 20 years for me to dig deeply enough to really take a look at why the marriage dissolved. Not that I hadn't asked myself a million times what triggered his unhappiness with our marriage. People would ask me,

"What happened?" I could honestly tell them I didn't know. It was only when I was willing and able to overcome my own ego, when I finally decided it was safe enough for me to understand the truth, that I had a breakthrough. The answer came when I was working through something entirely different. At least I thought it was entirely different.

You know some of this story already. To gain better perspective, I will fill in a few more of my life's details. My marriage felt "perfect," or so I thought. Others commented on how great it was to see a truly happy couple. Bob and I met in that modern dance group at a small liberal arts college. We began to fall in love over the next few months. Bob was and is a very talented guy. He danced, played a sweet guitar, taught me folk songs, and expressed his love for me in romantic ways that were endearing. It was the closest thing to perfection that I could imagine. By the following December we were engaged, and almost a year later we were married. I believed we were deeply in love and perfect for each other; I was 19.

As I wrote earlier, our first years of marriage were rough because Bob was drafted before we ever had a chance to learn how to be married. We lived through the ups and downs of being separated months at a time. We were uprooted and had to move five times in the first two years of our marriage. I never questioned our love for each other. We were living on romance. We both enjoyed acting in community theatre productions. We always loved to dance–modern, ballroom, disco, it didn't matter. When we danced, it felt like we were speaking our own language of love.

After his Army training, which took place over about five months, we were reunited. We lived just off the base at Fort Leonard Wood in Missouri. After a month of substitute teaching, I was hired by the local school district as attendance secretary. We desperately needed my income plus his military pay to cover our monthly bills. We joined the fort's community theatre group and began to make a few friends. We taught a dance class and performed in local productions. Suddenly everything changed again. Five months after our arrival at Fort Leonard Wood, he was headed to Seoul, Korea. Seven months later, I joined him in Seoul where I tutored those Korean students in Spoken American English.

After Korea, we returned to civilian life where we became active in our church, enjoyed acting, dancing and singing in plays and made new friends. Bob was able to return to the job he was drafted from and I finished college. I loved being with him. We never fought and rarely even disagreed. I thought our marriage was one of the happiest I had ever seen. I was reflecting what I believed to be true. I was in a happy marriage.

At some point, possibly after we celebrated our twelfth anniversary, things changed for Bob. Maybe it was even earlier than that, but I was not aware that he no longer loved me until then. If I had chosen to look carefully at our life together

I might have seen it sooner, but I believe my subconscious mind knew that not paying attention was safer.

I realized, much later, that I avoided exploring anything in our relationship that was unpleasant. One incident occurred when our daughter was born. We had planned a natural childbirth, but reality had a different plan. Amy's birth was an emergency caesarean section. At first the doctor induced labor. Six hours later, nothing was moving quickly and the doctor suggested it would be a while before anything would happen.

Looking back I can see how crazy it was to never have questioned why Bob decided to go home to sleep. I continued having painful but ineffective contractions and our baby's heartbeat was showing distress. About 1 AM, the doctor decided a C-section would be best. It would take place at 7:00 AM. They needed Bob to sign some forms. The nurse came in to ask me if my husband might have gone anyplace other than home. She had called our home number and there was no answer. I said, "No, but he is deaf and sleeps on his good ear so keep calling." She finally connected with him. I briefly saw him in the morning as they rolled me into surgery.

The next thing I remember I was in the recovery room waking from the general anesthetic, given then for C-sections. I heard the nurse call the pediatrician, who was a friend of ours. The doctor was at my side when I woke enough to understand his words, "You have a beautiful baby girl!" I was thrilled and wanted to share this time with Bob. But he had left the hospital after Amy was born. I later learned he had gone to work. For more than eight years, I never asked him why he went to work before I was out of recovery. That is a perfect example of my ego trying hard to protect me; "Don't ask, it's best not to know." I intuitively knew that asking questions like that could be the end of "perfection." It wasn't until "perfection" had completely ended that I allowed myself to even question that experience. By then I had cast myself as the heroic victim. I certainly needed a new casting director, but I didn't know that at the time.

After our daughter was born, we lived in what I experienced as happiness. Bob's career was moving along. After staying home with Amy for a couple of years, I began full-time work in my dream job, working with volunteers in a youth service organization. We were financially stable, enjoyed raising our daughter, active in community theatre and our church. Life was good. That was my reality. Moments that didn't fit that reality were quickly forgotten, ignored or forgiven and I made sure there weren't many of those moments!

But there came a time when I couldn't ignore his behavior. Although I didn't recognize this at the time, I later realized that when Bob and I disagreed, which wasn't often, I was always the one to say, "I'm sorry," whether I was at fault or not. One night I decided I would not apologize when I had done nothing wrong. For the first time in our marriage, I chose to sleep in another room. This went on for several nights as I waited for him to take responsibility for his behavior. As I walked out of our bedroom with my pillow and a blanket, I tweaked his toes and said, "It doesn't have to be this way." He didn't respond. I finally asked him if there was someone else. He said, "Yes."

That was the longest night of my life. I couldn't wait to call a friend who had been through a similar situation, to get the name of her therapist. I needed to talk to someone! Three months later Bob moved out and six weeks after that he said he wanted a divorce. Right up until that moment I believed we would end up back together and better than ever. But I believe that he was not happy from well before the argument he started. I simply couldn't see it. Even when I saw signs, I ignored them.

A few months after Bob told me he wanted a divorce he said, "Someday you will thank me for this." As unbelievable as it was at the time, he was right. I wouldn't know that for several years, but if he had not left me I would have continued creating the reality I believed existed, regardless of how damaging it might have been for me. If he had stayed, I would never have met and married my soul mate. I would never have experienced unconditional love. I would never have had even a fleeting glimpse of my life's purpose. I've never been sure what he meant when he said it. It doesn't matter, because what we hear and the meaning we choose to assign to any moment in our lives is what is important to us individually. Remember, this is me creating my reality, just as you create your reality.

Did I know then how to breathe into my inner wisdom? No. I had no idea. What I did have was a strong enough will to live through some very tough years. I had a very strong faith that there was something guiding and protecting me. I never stopped believing that something good would happen. I had hope. It may not be a strategy for some people but it was a lifesaving tool. I would need and use it over and over.

Fast-forward almost 30 years and there I was finding myself the losing partner in another long-term relationship. This time it was with my company's client. In my mind there was a cast of characters who were the "evildoers" and others who were the "angels" and I cast myself as the victim – again! This is the story I began this book with and used as a caution to "be careful what you wish for" in Chapter 5. Now it serves as an example of gaining perspective, which can take years.

I had served as the executive director for the local chamber of commerce for almost 18 years. The relationship was rather unique. Step back in time 16 years. The Chamber was relatively new, in financial red ink and without professional leadership. I was approached by one of the volunteer board members asking if I would be interested in a part-time position as executive director. I knew immediately I did not want to be someone's employee. My business partner Penny and I had left Chrysler and opened our new business a little more than two years before. I talked with Penny about the possibility of suggesting we take the chamber on as a client. We would provide all of the services an executive director and staff would normally provide including office space (our office) and the chamber would pay us a monthly fee. After three months of negotiations, a letter of agreement was signed.

Earlier I mentioned the letter of agreement that was revised every year or two as we renegotiated our relationship. Over those years the chamber thrived; I loved the work and the relationships we built with the members. The economic downturn began in Michigan in 2001. The first large automotive layoffs began when one of the Big 3 merged with another company. The chamber's membership began a very slow decline as automotive suppliers went out of business, and then a few years later the suppliers to the suppliers began to close their doors. Each year we thought the local economy would begin to recover, but it didn't. That affected membership and, by 2008, the Chamber's leadership created a committee to look for creative ways to address membership decline. By this time, Penny had retired.

In the wake of declining membership, a committee was formed to develop creative marketing strategies to increase membership and improve the bottom line. I was surprised to learn the committee began its search by questioning the relationship between my company and the chamber. It felt like a betrayal. Sixteen years of dedicated, professional work led to year after year of increased growth, until recently. The chamber had a good, strong reputation according to many of our members and the other local chambers. That was what I was concentrating on at the time. The committee's focus, however, was on the present, not the past.

There was clumsy handling of the situation on both sides. When I was abruptly asked to leave a board meeting so the board could discuss our agreement, I was surprised. Thirty-five minutes later, I still had not been asked to return to the meeting. My fear disguised as anger was mounting. I saw board members leaving. All but one left without saying a word to me. I was confused and insulted. The remaining board member told me three of the members would meet with me privately later in the week. All I could think of was that, once again, I wasn't wanted. I certainly didn't connect the dots until months later; but my ego recognized the experience and decided the best defense is a good offense.

I was hurt by what I saw as personal assaults on my work and insults regarding my ability. Years later, with perspective, I could see how I could have reacted differently. Then I was reacting out of fear–fear of the loss of one of our biggest clients, fear in a time that marked not only the decline of the auto industry, but the entire national economy. All I had invested in the past 18 years would dissolve, and it did. But I was determined to make the decisions this time. I would dissolve the relationship between my company and our client. I felt like the victim, but it was a reality I created for myself. A reality I created by acting from fear.

The amazing thing to me is that I was not aware of the part I was playing in this chapter of my life. At first I tried to use reason and facts. I prepared a PowerPoint presentation for the board outlining the entire role my company had played in the chamber's early history and later success, as well as the membership growth and program development we were responsible for. That seemed to go well. But shortly afterward, I was getting feedback that certain board members were adamant that a change was needed. After my initial attempt to see reason, I veered off into defense mode.

There were some board members who tried to help but I was unable to stop my "pre-programmed" reaction. In my divorce, 30 years previously, I simply let my husband do what he wanted to do. That hadn't worked too well for me. This time I would take charge and end the relationship on my terms. I would do the leaving.

I don't know if the outcome would have been any different if I had known how to Breathe Into Wisdom, but I am certain the process would have been more graceful and certainly less fear-filled. I had an important life lesson to learn and the universe believed I was ready.

My company's relationship with the chamber had come to an end. My company of twenty years was closing its doors. As I turned out the lights for the last time and locked the doors, I felt only exhaustion. Rest and two years' time would give me the perspective I would need to make sense of what had happened.

Perspective is an amazing thing. It does not come from being "in" an experience. It doesn't come from living in the moment, although it can inform how we live in our moments. It comes from having lived through them. By that I mean, after an experience, joy-filled or angst-filled, at some point in the future you are able to look back and see that experience from a different point of view. It might have been a wonderful experience that led to great happiness. With perspective you fully understand how that single moment changed your life, leading you down a path of great fulfillment until something bad happens. Then you forget the beauty and joy of the moment and only focus on what you don't have, didn't experience, and didn't receive. Maybe you act from fear.

It could be a gut-wrenching experience that tears your life apart. You may feel victimized. Or your life has been ruined because of some person or event or series of events. With the perspective of time, you may still feel you want revenge. You may still feel the victim. Or you might see how that experience and those people presented you with an opportunity to find encouragement to move forward. You choose to pick yourself up, to no longer play the part of a victim. You gather all of the lessons that might be helpful to you in the future and you move to a better place in your understanding of that experience. You consciously begin to create your own reality! Eventually I found myself on that path.

Examine Your Own Perspective

What lesson resonated with you as you read this chapter? Do you have an experience or two or three that, when strung together, create a life pattern? Have you experienced a time when you ignored the wonder and joy in your life and chose to focus on what you didn't have? Are you possibly, even at this moment, playing the victim in your own life story?

Take a few minutes to close your eyes and breathe deeply into your own wisdom. Breathe slowly, deep into your belly, letting your breath touch the back of your throat and ask Spirit or God or Wisdom what were you supposed to learn from those experiences?

Sit quietly and continue to breathe slowly, deeply in through your nose and then slowly release your breath through your lips, blowing gently. Feel the intake of breath on the back of your throat as you ask Wisdom your questions. Continue as you reflect on your experiences. Relax; there is no hurry, no expectation, no right or wrong, just you connecting to Wisdom.

Ask Spirit questions that may lead to answers of inspiration. This is not the time to ask "why" questions but "how" questions. For example, how might I look at this differently? How can I use this experience for my highest and best good? How will taking this step lead me to my life purpose? "How" questions help you learn to think differently about an issue. They help you imagine new and different methods to use when you explore a situation, a relationship or a challenge.

Understand that constantly shaping your reality with your thoughts is a practice. The more we practice breathing as a meditation, the easier it becomes to accept that we have some control over what our thoughts are. Let's take a look at what we do with our experiences shapes our reality.

Part Three

Breathe

Chapter 10

Creating Your Own Reality

No, I didn't make the board members behave in any particular way. No, I didn't lob the first volley. No, I had not asked for any of this to happen ... or had I?

After Bob left me, it took 30 years to gain the perspective I needed to understand I was not a victim. His leaving, as sad and painful as it was for me, opened my understanding of possibility. I had never thought about getting an M.B.A. before I became a single parent. I would never have imagined the experiences life presented me, both good and bad, working at Chrysler. I would probably never have owned my own business. All of those life experiences resulted from the reality that Bob and I created by allowing our relationship to end in divorce and my subsequent choices.

Now it was my business relationship that had ended. This time I played the victim for less than two years. I was beginning to understand more about creating my own reality. By simply shifting my attitude about what had happened, I could see how the end of that relationship opened up space for me to live the life I wanted. You might think two years is a long time, and it is when you are living it. But, looking back, in the scheme of things, two years was a lot better than 30 years! I was beginning to be a quick study.

But how did I even begin to know there could be a different way to live in this life? How did I get started? It began with the internet. Yes, the internet. One day I received what might have been spam; but it wasn't. It was an email from Adam King. He was offering a program he called The Tessera Method. I am, even now, surprised I bought his offering. But I am glad I did. Adam provided my entry into a community I didn't even know existed. One where I could learn to get "outside the box" of what I could experience with my five senses. I had always believed in a sixth sense but I certainly had never been exposed to it in the way Adam's Tessera offered. I began to "see" my future work. It would be filled with retreats and teaching. This was well before the dissolution of my company. The seed had been planted that there might be a different way to understand life.

In the last chapter I talked about the disappointment of losing one of my company's largest clients after an 18-year relationship. But the reality was that I didn't lose the relationship, I ended it. It took me two years of deep grief to gain that understanding.

Two years of ruminating, rehashing conversations in my head every night as I tried to go to sleep. I thought about how I would respond differently to questions about the value my company delivered to the chamber over the years. I imagined having a conversation with particular board members to help them see where their thinking was flawed. But that day I described in Chapter 3, when I sat in the small garage-type storage unit where the office furniture, file cabinets and files were stored, a strange thing happened. It was a sunny Michigan August day. The door to the unit was wide open, the sun was streaming down on me as I moved from the file cabinets to the paper shredder. I was ready to get rid of everything I would not need again. I was shredding old financial statements, duplicate copies of completed projects, old project proposals. I was shredding memories.

After twenty years as a small business owner I knew every client, project, invoice, and payment we had received. I relived the hundreds of events we produced, newsletters we had written, research conducted. So much of it had been good work, sometimes groundbreaking. For me the relationships we created were the most precious products of those 20 years. Maybe that was what hurt the most about the Chamber experience. The day-to-day relationships with both corporate employees and entrepreneurs were gone.

As I sorted, I was struck by a thought. I had gotten what I wanted. What? How could that be? Was I delusional? After two years of trying to hold on to the business before it ended, and two more years of enduring what felt like great loss, how had I gotten what I wanted? Here's how.

In 2001, my sister Jane retired after 30 years of teaching. In 2007 my business partner Penny retired. Michael was retired. My brother-in-law Greg was retired from his business. Although I was younger than all of them I would tell people, "I sure wish I could retire." I said it often. I thought it often. I knew I couldn't retire until I reached my 66th birthday and that was several years away. But I loved the idea of doing just what I wanted to do, when I wanted to do it. It wasn't that I didn't want to work any longer, I just wanted to work in a different way, doing what I believe I am here to do. That was what retirement looked like to me. I didn't think I could give up my income yet, but I so wanted that time to come.

Wishing for something and getting it are two different things! As I sat in the storage unit with the sun shining down on me I realized that the Universe had provided me with exactly what I had asked for. I was retired. Never mind that our income had been pretty much eliminated. Ignore the fact that I had no health insurance. Forget the part about doing what I wanted to do when I wanted to do it. Why hadn't I repeated those things over and over each time I said, "I wish I could retire." Yikes! I was retired. I had created my own reality.

When the opportunity presented itself – the chamber committee simply questioned their largest annual expenditure, which was to pay my company to manage and house their organization – I leapt to the conclusion they wanted to get rid of ME! Well it wasn't exactly like that. There were allegations by members of the committee questioning the legality of the relationship. Questions arose about the chamber finally increasing their monthly payments to include their use of our office space for chamber business. My company had covered all of those expenses for 15 years without compensation. When the chamber seemed strong enough to cover those costs, one of the board members moved that a substantial increase be included in our Letter of Agreement. The following year was when the questions of the legality of the relationship surfaced. So I wasn't delusional in feeling a bit blindsided by some of the comments and questions, but I was beginning to gain a little perspective.

With that perspective came the realization I had, in fact, created the reality I repeatedly asked for! I was retired, except I wasn't. The same day I dissolved the Sub-chapter S Corporation, I went directly to the County offices and opened a dba (doing business as) called SKR Coaching & Consulting. I was creating a business that was exactly what my heart had yearned to do forever. I wanted to help people create the lives they desired. The perspective of two years allowed me to see clearly that what I had said I wanted was now mine.

Looking back, I began to see time after time how my perspective created my reality. As far back as when Bob and I were in Korea, I could recall various experiences that confirmed I had been creating my own reality all my life – and so are you! I even learned that the perspective doesn't have to take years to come into focus. It might only take moments for your perspective to change. For example you may be traveling along in life, relaxed and happy, and suddenly you are in a terrifying situation you never expected to face. In fact, you couldn't have created the reality because you didn't even know such a possibility could exist.

I was 21 years old, living with Bob in Seoul, Korea. As you learned in Chapter 2, when I joined Bob in Korea, the Civil Service job I expected was no longer available. I did, without realizing it, continue my relentless journey of overcoming obstacles in my own way. I lived in Seoul for seven months. During that time I attracted 16 students whom I met with several times a week. Some came to our apartment to be tutored. I met some in their own homes or work locations. When I met away from my home, the student usually sent a car to pick me up and deliver me home again.

On one occasion I chose to take the public bus, just as an adventure. On this particular day I was traveling without anyone who could translate for me. I was trying out my newly learned Korean phrases. When the bus arrived I asked the "bus girl" if this bus went to DeHan Kukjong, which was my attempt to say Korean movie theatre. "Ne, Ne," she said. Yes. Great, it is the right bus! I got on and off we went.

When, after a 20-minute ride, I realized I was not seeing anything familiar, it occurred to me I was going to be late for my class. After 45 minutes, I knew I was not on the right bus. Not recognizing anything I saw and with more bus passengers leaving at every stop, I became worried. Finally, after more than an hour, I was the only passenger left on the bus. The driver pulled into a lot, turned off the bus and motioned for me to get out. I had no idea where I was. No one spoke English, except me, and it was pretty clear I didn't speak Korean! I disembarked into a cold, blustery February winter day.

As usual, I had almost no money. I brought only enough for my round trip bus fare, about the equivalent of 10 cents, to travel from home to my student's condo in downtown Seoul and back to Nam Yong Dong. I stepped off the bus in a dirt parking lot and began to walk along an almost deserted street. The wind whipped through my wool coat, my feet were instantly cold, my face stung from the frozen rain hitting it. Soon the tears began to trickle down my cheeks. I had no idea where I was. I knew I was no longer in the city. I saw what looked like small factories, vacant land, and, in the distance, farmland. I had no idea how to tell anyone what had happened. I couldn't even find a building that might have a telephone, and if I had I would not know how to ask if I might make a call. The bravery I usually felt at times like this had disappeared when I left the bus. I had no idea how to get home! Fear started to find a place in my head and my heart. What would happen to me?

I passed a few people and asked if they spoke English. No one did. They hurried along, never looking back. I was truly alone. After about 20 minutes of walking first one way on the dirt street and then back on the other side, a man appeared from behind a fence. He was filthy, covered in dirt and wearing somewhat ragged clothing. He motioned to me to come into the fenced area. Although I was afraid, I had no other options that looked any better.

I followed him. Then he motioned for me to enter a small shack. That called for more courage than I had ever needed. Even more frightening, when I entered I saw the faces of four or five other men dressed exactly as the first man – equally as dirty and ragged – looking furtively at me. My heart was pounding; no one would ever find me. What were these men planning? There was only one window and no light. The men were warming themselves around a charcoal stove. There was a bench and a table on the wall opposite the men.

It was at that moment the first man pointed to a telephone sitting on the table. His look gave me permission to use the phone. I had no idea how he knew what I needed, there were no windows facing the street in the shack so he couldn't have seen me from there. But he and the other men knew I needed help and they could at least offer a form of communication.

I only had one number I could call. It was the number to the two-bedroom apartment we shared with another couple. Usually no one was home during the day except Miss Kim, the maid who came with the apartment, and me. Today I got lucky. For some reason, Larry, one of our apartment mates, answered the phone. I told him what had happened and that I had only enough money for one bus fare. He told me what to ask for when I found another bus. He added that I could ask for a transfer and my ticket would allow me to travel on the second bus at no additional charge. That second bus would deliver me to within two blocks of our apartment.

The men smiled – they no longer looked frightening. Those furtive looks had simply been the shyness of working Korean men being in close proximity to a young American woman. In fact, they looked like angels. I respectfully nodded my head in a downward direction and went back outside with one of the men who showed me where to stand to catch a bus. When a bus arrived I asked for the R.K.O train station where I would be able to get a transfer ticket. I followed Larry's directions and arrived home safely.

What began as an adventure had turned into a complete sense of being lost and afraid. By now the fear had transformed back into an adventure of a very different sort. I created the entire reality by what I believed. I believed I could find my way around Seoul. I believed the bus would at least return eventually to where I started. When I had to get off the bus, I believed I would find someone to help me, but quickly I lost my belief and became afraid. Once I was afraid, everything frightened me. The lack of help, the dirty man in the ragged clothes, the shack filled with other dirty ragged men – all of this was my created reality. Then, when the man pointed to the phone and smiled his toothless grin, my reality shifted again. Although I still felt fear that no one would be home to answer the call, I knew those men meant me no harm.

Finally, once my "escort" saw me safely to the right bus, my reality shifted out of fear and into curiosity and hope that I would make it home safely. What message does this story have about creating my own reality? It is a snapshot of how quickly what we believe is happening to us can change. Moment by moment we tell ourselves stories about what is happening. This is one part of how we create our own reality.

We believe ourselves. We tell ourselves we know what is happening. We create a frame of reference we understand to be true until something happens to change our understanding. We are not always conscious of this but when you look at the clock you might think, "I have plenty of time." That is your current reality. The phone rings, you answer it. The call takes longer than you expect. Now your reality requires you to rush – you are now late. That is your new reality. You may say, "Of course, that IS the reality." But it is only <u>your</u> reality if you believe it. How can I say that? Because it is true.

This is a simplification of the process of creating your own reality but it is accurate to say, "what you think creates your reality." Let's look at an example. You have a meeting scheduled for two o'clock and you like to arrive early. Travel time is 15 minutes. If you are a person who believes the traffic is always heavy you may leave at 1:30 and arrive 10 minutes early. You believe you are right on time!

Another person leaving for the same meeting with the same expected travel time leaves at 1:45 and walks into the meeting, sits down and the meeting begins. He feels he is right on time.

A third person, attending the same meeting, arrives just in time to be introduced to the other people at the meeting and breathes with a sigh of relief – "Right on time!" For each person their reality is that they arrived "right on time." What we believe creates our reality.

You might be thinking, "Fine. I get that." You identify with one of the three scenarios. Take this understanding and apply it to a more complicated scenario. Each of these people held a certain belief about "being on time." That belief was what created comfort for them to arrive when they did. That was their reality. But if all three of the people switched places in time of arrival they would have claimed a different reality.

The first person would have arrived only in time to be introduced would have believed he was "late." The second person would have arrived 10 minutes early and might have found it uncomfortable to make small talk. The third person, arriving as the meeting was just beginning would have held a reality of arriving with "a little time to spare."

How does this simple series of scenarios relate to how you create your reality? What you think about, what you believe to be true about everything that happens to you creates your reality. If you like your reality you don't have to change a thing right now. But if you are unhappy with your reality, if you would like to make a change or a series of changes, you can – in other words; you are able to change your reality. Or, more specifically, you may change your perception of your reality. Because it is your perception that matters to you, just as every other person's perception matters to him or her.

This is only the first step in creating your own reality. When I believed I had to go back to school to support my daughter and myself when Bob left, I created that reality. There might have been several other scenarios I could have chosen, but I chose to believe I needed another degree to make "enough" money. So I went to graduate school, got the degree and secured a job. Later I would see that was probably not what I was supposed to do. The job did not make my heart sing, but it did put food on the table and a roof over our heads.

Later I would learn about living my life on purpose. I was discovering how powerful I was in creating my own reality.

Take a moment right now to breathe deeply into your own understanding of what you just read.

1. **Close your eyes, breathe in deeply through your nose letting your breath hit the back of your throat.**
2. **Slowly release the breath through your mouth.**
3. **Take another deep, slow breath following the same technique, but concentrate on feeling the breath reach into your belly.**
4. **Relax. If you can't feel it the first few times, keep working on breathing into your belly slowly and easily, hold the breath for a moment and then let your breath out slowly through your mouth – ahhh.**
5. **As you practice, it will become second nature to breathe like this when you are ready to connect to your spirit.**

Allow yourself at least ten minutes of uninterrupted time to do the following exercise:

As you breathe in, slowly and deeply, bring to mind something you wish was different in your life. It can be a relationship, a health issue, a financial situation, a living arrangement; it could be anything you would like to change. For this exercise, it may take a while to decide which issue you want to concentrate on. Take your time. This won't be your only chance and you can change the issue if you begin the exercise and decide this is not the one you want to concentrate on. In other words, give yourself complete permission to move along as it feels right, without any judgment.

Read through the following first, then close your eyes and follow the steps:

1. Close your eyes; select an issue to concentrate on.
2. Breathe in slowly, deeply through your nose, deep into your belly. Try to feel the breath against the back of your throat. Then breathe out slowly blowing through your lips.
3. Do this a few times until you are relaxed.
4. Begin to think about your issue of concentration. My example here will be a relationship.
5. Think about the relationship. Who or what is the other part of the relationship? What is the difficulty, friction, dissatisfaction, fear? Just sit with those questions for a few minutes while you continue to breathe.
6. Ask yourself, your spirit, your God, whatever you feel comfortable with, "What is causing my distress with this situation?" Again, there is no hurry. Just keep breathing slowly and be alert to any thought you have. It doesn't matter if you actually "think" the words or if an answer seems to develop. Just

be with the question, "What is causing my distress with ....?" You may think or realize nothing. That's fine. Just sit with the question. Keep breathing.

7. You might take a different approach to the question. Ask, "Is there something else that may play a part in my distress?" then possibly "Is there another way I could look at this situation?" "How else might I approach this?"

8. If you find yourself emotionally uncomfortable, you are likely digging deeply and I encourage you to release all judgment. Just keep breathing and concentrating. Your breath should be relaxed and your thoughts might be coming more quickly now. The last question you might ask is, "Is this understanding in my highest and best good?" In other words, "Am I creating my best life when I understand the situation this way?" If you feel a "yes," great. If not, you might want to continue the exercise.

9. You may stop at one of two points: either when you have reached what I call an "aha!" or when you feel there is nothing new coming through your mind.

10. When you are ready to stop, slowly move your head, wiggle your fingers and toes, take one last deep breath in, blow it out and slowly open your eyes.

Congratulations, you have just completed your first step to breathing into your Wisdom.

The first time I experienced this type of breathing, I was focusing on finances. I actually began to piece together some old stories that I had absorbed in early childhood. I told you about my great aunt in Chapter 2 when I used EFT (Emotional Freedom Tapping) to reach into my childlike understanding that wealthy people are very unhappy and unkind. This time I wanted to use breathing to ask how I could attract financial abundance. By the third or fourth time I concentrated on my inability to attract abundance, I realized I had connected wealth with unkind and unhappy people. Those are two things I have never wanted to be in my life. So I chose not to attract abundance because, in my unconscious self, being kind and happy were more important to me than having a financially abundant life.

Bringing that kind of understanding to the conscious level then allowed me to adjust my conscious attitude. Now I am consciously remembering to welcome abundance of all kinds into my life. I am often surprised at how that part of my life is improving.

If you have access to the internet just log on to *www.skrcoaching.com* and click on the **Breathe Into Wisdom** window where you can not only share your experience but click on Breath Meditation 2 where you will hear me lead you through this exercise. I look forward to hearing how this experience touches your life

Breathe

Chapter 11

Set Your Intention

There I was, a newly minted M.B.A. and a new Chrysler employee. I arrived for my first day of work to learn that I had a desk, but my supervisor was out of the building and would not return until 11:00 AM. He left a few forms for me to fill out. I completed those in a few minutes. I had three hours until I learned what my job would entail. I was supposed to see the company doctor for a physical at 10:00 AM. Until then, I decided to write a list of goals for my Chrysler career. It was 1985. Over the next 45 minutes or so I created five years of salary and grade goals for myself. I put the list in my desk drawer. Back in Chapter 4, I mentioned making this list and promised we would get back to it in this chapter. Over the next five years and three months, that paper would be moved each time I moved to a new position. My first move took place six months later when the list was tucked in a box and I never reviewed it, never even looked at it until I left Chrysler in 1990.

When I was emptying my desk as I prepared to leave Chrysler and start my own business with my business partner, Penny, I found that original list. As I looked at the short list, only six lines long followed by my signature and the date, I was astounded to see that I had written my salary amounts for each year from 1986 through 1990. But I had written them in 1985! I had not looked at the paper to see what it said at any time during those years. But each year when I went through my review and was given my raise, if I had looked at the list I would have seen the exact amount my manager offered me. Coincidence? For five years in a row? Not very likely.

The most interesting part of this story is that I never updated that list. I never extended it beyond those five years. I distinctly remember being surprised at how un-excited I felt when my manager in 1990 told me I would become eligible for a lease car and a raise that would put me at the last salary I had written on my list. I knew that day I was going to have to leave. I could no longer work in the environment that was killing my soul. Did I somehow "know" in 1985 I wouldn't be there more than five years? I don't think so. I had high hopes that first day back in 1985. But within six weeks, I knew I had made a serious mistake in accepting the job. I didn't belong in that kind of corporate environment. But the lessons I learned over those years prepared me well for the work that lay ahead in co-owning my own business for the next 20 years.

That was some powerful list making! This next one resulted in the most beautiful change I have experienced.

Remember the marriage counselor who invited Bob and me to list the things that were important to us in a mate? I spent a great deal of time working on my list. I went into great detail about the type of relationship I wanted with not only my husband but his family as well. I wanted someone who would love me as much as I loved him. Someone who was intelligent and kind and thoughtful and had a good sense of humor. Someone who wouldn't be easily upset and with whom it would be a joy to share my life. Someone who could love my daughter. The list was almost a full page, hand-written, single spaced. I took this exercise very seriously. As I recall, when we shared our lists there were no matching items between Bob's list and mine. I put the list in a drawer and didn't read it again until six years later when Michael and I were about to be married.

I was clearing out drawers in a bedroom dresser for him to use and I came across the "wish list." To my utter amazement and delight I realized I was marrying the man I described in my list six years earlier!

I didn't connect the full importance of lists until a few years later. I was teaching a class and I asked the participants if they ever wrote down what they wanted to happen in their lives. In trying to illustrate why I believe making lists is important, I actually shared the "what I wanted in a mate" story. After I left Chrysler and was teaching again, I added the story about the salary list I made. Since then I have often included the idea that making a list of your intentions is very important to achieving them. In fact, almost every curriculum I created over the next 20 years included that point. I still believe making lists is a surefire way to get what you hope for.

How does that work? I believe it fits beautifully with my understanding that the Universe is always conspiring for my highest and best good. It does that for anyone who asks. Those last two sentences are worth re-reading. The Universe is <u>always</u> <u>conspiring</u> for your highest and best good. It does that for anyone who asks. In other words, if you know what you want, really want, and you are willing to do what it takes to get it, the Universe will do everything to help you achieve your goal – as long as it is in your highest and best good. I didn't get to keep my first marriage together, but I was now married to a man who was everything I could have wished for on that list and more. For almost 30 years I have enjoyed the benefits of taking that list-making seriously!

An important life lesson is: clearly set your own intentions for the important things in your life. You need to know what you want. If you don't, you will find it hard to know if you get it. You may find yourself following paths that lead to dead ends. You won't know which fork in the road to take in decision-making. You won't know if you are getting closer to achieving what you want because you haven't determined what it is you want.

Another experience of setting intention, which doesn't involve writing a list, occurred while I was still in the corporate world. I was miserable in the Information Technology area. Luckily, by now, I had a wonderful boss. He hired me knowing I had no programming experience. He hired me for my strengths – writing and training. When I was assigned the task of writing speeches for various executives, I enjoyed interviewing the speakers to learn what message they wanted to deliver. They seemed satisfied with my work, which felt rewarding. It's a tricky business to write words that will come out of someone else's mouth!

When I was training in the classroom, I felt my spirit soar. I loved to help people learn how to get along and how to create environments that could be productive with the least amount of stress and failure. I knew that my being there made a difference for many of the participants in class.

But there were 40 hours in a week to fill and often I would be expected to actually write computer programs. I had almost no idea what I was doing. Since I was at the bottom of the ladder, there were many layers of programmers between my work and the end result. During one of those weeks when I was trying to write a program, I must have expressed my discontent once too often and a little too loudly.

A woman sitting across the aisle from me asked me what I would really like to do. I told her I liked to write and train. She thought for a few minutes and said, "Do you know about the Women's Leadership Network?" I had never heard of it. She said, "You need to attend a meeting and meet a woman named Penny Manning. I don't know what she does but I think it has to do with marketing and she works for Chrysler in the Troy office. She might be able to help you." I lived in Troy at the time and marketing sounded a lot better than computer programming!

That was in September. The Women's Leadership Network met once a month. I don't enjoy attending dinner meetings by myself. So, true to my nature, which is to organize group activities, I spent a few weeks telling other women at work about this group. By November I had five other women interested in attending a meeting. I learned that Glenda Greenwald, wife of Chrysler's Executive Vice President, the company we all worked for, was going to speak at the January meeting. Perfect! We all made reservations for the dinner.

That evening I arrived with my friends. I was circulating, looking for a woman with a nametag that read "Penny Manning."

I shook a lot of hands and wondered if maybe this wasn't my night. We were told the buffet line was open so I got in line. I was chatting with the woman behind me. Then I turned forward as the woman in front of me turned, put out her hand and said, "Hello, I'm Penny Manning." I responded, "Hello, I'm Susan Rothfuss and I am here to meet you tonight." She laughed and asked why. I told her about the woman who directed me to this meeting and why. She asked what I was good at, I told her, "writing and training." I gave her my card and she said she would be in touch.

The next day she called and asked me to send my PHR (Personnel History Record) and resume to her; she would pass it on to her boss. About two weeks later, I was interviewing for a job in Service Contracts Marketing. Penny helped make it happen. As you read these words, know that 27 years later we are still in touch and very good friends. We were co-workers for a little more than two years at Chrysler, then decided to go into business together. We were business partners for 17 years, until her retirement. Since then we have maintained a close friendship and she is a trusted advisor.

All of that came from setting an intention for one evening, to meet Penny Manning. I don't remember the name of the contract programmer who made the suggestion, but I am very thankful she did.

Now, if you will notice, in each story I told you, I either created a list with intentions or I set an intention. These are only a few examples of the many times I have used this technique to achieve a desired outcome. I'll admit I chose the most important times to tell you about. What I may not have emphasized is that not only did I set the intention, I put in the work it took to finish the job. In other words, I put the intention out there AND then, despite being hurt by my divorce, I was open to meeting Michael; I worked hard at Chrysler for five years to earn those salaries; and I showed up at the Women's Leadership Network dinner to meet Penny.

So as important as it is to make a list of what you want, you can't sit back and just expect it to happen. That reminds me of a conversation a minister and I were having years ago. I mentioned a difficult parishioner and asked how she dealt with a particular situation where this person was concerned. She said, "Sometimes I say to God, 'I know it's all in Your hands, but couldn't you at least give me a little something to work with!'" We both laughed. Sometimes it feels as though we have nothing to work with. I had no marriage left, but I was willing to make the list. I couldn't see a way out of the IT Department, but I heard that one voice asking "What do you like to do?" and I responded.

In other words, be open to possibility. You never know where it will turn up, what it will look or sound like or where it will lead. Always set your intention, know what it is you want to explore, ask, learn, and know. At this point you might be asking, "What does this have to do with breathing into wisdom?" To which I respond, "A lot."

Whether you sense your wisdom coming directly from your own spirit, or from the source of your life by whatever name you choose to call it, you have a font of wisdom from which you can draw at any time. That source doesn't need to hear your words, but you need to say them to understand what your deepest desire is. Your source knows before you utter a word what you want or need. That is why I believe the universe is conspiring for our highest and best good. Because wisdom is available but not intrusive – it is up to you to ask.

By making your lists, whether in your head or on paper, you are directly connecting your Source with your desire. When you breathe deeply into your center and connect with your Source, you set aside the obstacles of your life and communicate with the power that can help you achieve your goals. What might seem a simple task, making a list, becomes a powerful tool when filled with intention. By focusing your thoughts on what you would like to draw into your life, you are creating thoughts that flow into the subconscious and continue to work with Spirit to achieve your goals until the desired result occurs.

Do you have your own list already or would you like to create one? Some people refer to their "Bucket List." This became popular after the movie of the same name came out. It is used to describe all the things you most want to experience before you leave this life. Having one list is not enough for me. I have found it helpful to make a list each time I have a big goal or a seemingly impossible dream to achieve. Imagine what you could accomplish if you connected to the source that is conspiring for your highest and best good.

Having said that, it is important to remember that what you want most may not be in your highest and best good. As humans we do not have the ability to see for ourselves what our futures hold, at least not yet. For example when my first husband wanted a divorce, I couldn't know that a much greater love would present itself in the form of Michael. But my source knew there were better things to come. I wasn't sure I could even live through the loss, let alone imagine something better. At the time I didn't know enough to even ask if better was possible. I thought I had already had the best. The Universe had good news for me!

When I was living through the challenging times at Chrysler, I did know enough to wake up each morning and say, "God, what am I supposed to learn from this today?" My heart held a hope that something good would come. And indeed it did, in the form of a business I could call my own.

By the time I closed TMD Consulting, I was deeply sad, scared and unsure of what the future would bring. But I knew I could move forward. I had experienced a "knowing" that went beyond my own brainpower by experiencing Adam King's Tessera Method. But I didn't know I could simply breathe into that wisdom. The more I learned and experienced things that took me beyond my five senses, the more I knew there was to learn. To do that I had to practice.

Practicing is something we inherently know to do. When my grandchildren were babies I watched them consider making sounds and first words; I could see how hard they concentrated. They wanted to talk. The same was true with learning to walk. When I took piano as a child, practicing was a chore. I am not a gifted musician, although I have always loved music. I wasn't able to make the connection between my goal of playing well and the hours and hours of boring practice it would take to reach that goal. As an adult I sit down to "practice" many times a day. I am still not gifted, but I love to hear the sonatinas develop as I finally find the right notes played in the correct time to actually make music. When we are practicing something we really want to become proficient at, we eagerly practice. We try over and over and over until we achieve our goals.

Before we can practice, we need to describe our goal – being shy, you want to meet a mate or you are tired of your dead-end job and you want to find meaningful work -- write down, as specifically as you can, what you want. If you know there are several steps to reach the goal, list each step. I encourage you to do that now. Begin by Breathing Into Wisdom, asking for guidance and honesty with yourself. While making the list, be as specific as you feel comfortable. If you can't decide which part of your life to start with, just pick one and know when that list is finished you can write another. Once the list is written, you don't have to refer to it daily or even regularly. The items should be long-term rather than short-term goals. It is important to keep the list so, at some point in the future you can look at it with amazement and gratitude to the universe!

Now it's time to seriously set your intention on learning more, every day, about what this life is about. When I decided to do that, I had no idea where it would lead, but I was ready to practice, practice, practice.

Chapter 12

Practice, Practice, Practice!

When we begin something new we might have a natural talent for it, or we might not have any idea what we are doing. The same is true for us as we begin a process of transformation. To discuss transformation, we need an agreed-upon vocabulary so we can understand what we are talking about. Here are a few key words and the definitions I assign to them.

Spirit – That part of us that is our essence. It is with us and is older than our bodies. Your spirit knows what your life is to be about and its purpose, even when your mind doesn't have a clue! Your spirit is endlessly generous to you and through you.

Transformation – Changing from one thing or form to another. The change may be an intellectual belief, a spiritual belief or a physical change. When you have a strong opinion and you hear something that challenges that opinion, you might listen and think about the new information. Then some experience challenges your strongly held belief. Possibly a third or fourth fact or experience is presented and you realize your understanding is changing. That is the process of transformation at work.

Ego – A Freudian term described in Merriam Webster's New World Dictionary as, "… the part of the psyche that experiences the external world or reality, through the senses, organizes the thought processes rationally and governs action."[16] In Spiritual terms the ego is often referred to as "monkey brain" or the place where "monkey talk" originates. It is the part of the brain that tries to protect you from being hurt – physically or psychologically.

Those three terms cover a lot of territory when I talk about making changes in our lives that will transform us.

In Chapter 3, I shared the path I took on my own Spiritual Journey that began with the Spiritual Formation group at my church. I wrote about the Interfaith Service on National Day of Prayer where I was moved to deeply question all divisions between people. In Chapter 3, you will also find the list of books I read to learn more about other religions and cultures.

My transformation began with a niggling around my interpretation of my religion. As the years passed and I learned more about the similarities among all of Earth's major religions, I realized I could no longer subscribe to one. Ten years or so after that beautiful National Day of Prayer experience, I became a Unitarian Universalist. I found a church with a faith tradition that draws from many different faith traditions, in the belief that no one religion has all the answers and that most have something to teach us. It is a non-creedal church.

That is a brief example of a personal transformation. It reflects my transformation from a traditional Christian believer to a person who understands that I am a spirit having a human experience. My belief can be stated simply. I believe I came from love. I live in love. When my body dies, I will return to love. I am a spirit. My body is the vehicle I use to navigate this life and it brings me great joy and sometimes pain through my physical senses. This is my current understanding. I accept it may not be so in the future. That is a fertile mindset that allows for transformation as I evolve.

The previous five paragraphs briefly describe what took years of my life to achieve. During those years I stayed open to seeing, hearing, learning, accepting and developing new ideas. It became a personal practice of mine to imagine possibility. When I first began, I didn't even know I was developing a practice.

First I wanted to learn more. Then I was exposed to the interfaith service. Then I realized I couldn't learn enough by doing the same thing over and over, so I took one entire year and each week I visited a different house of worship. That was a challenge since so much of my social life was connected to my Presbyterian Church on Sunday mornings. Sometimes when I actually drove past my church to attend a service with people I had never met, I yearned to turn into the familiar parking lot! But I had a commitment to myself to learn something new and so I drove on.

During that year I learned so much. I allowed myself to be awash in the awareness that I simply didn't know what I didn't know, but I could learn. I tested many of my long-held beliefs within my own mind and experience. I let go of some, while others still serve me well. These beliefs are not religious in nature, but spiritual. I began to trust what my heart had to say. On the way I learned about the brain, the ego, and the rational world's answers. That began with the wonderful book I introduced you to in Chapter 8 by Dr. Jill Bolte Taylor, *My Stroke of Insight.* I highly recommend it to anyone who wants to stretch his or her understanding of what is possible.

At the age of 37, this Harvard-trained brain scientist experienced a stroke and she writes about her stroke and complete recovery. In a few hours she went from being a neuroanatomist to an infant in a woman's body. Her recovery took years, but throughout the process she learned important things about her own brain and how it functions. Her left brain was damaged during the stroke. The left brain handles critical thinking, makes judgments, and processes information at lightning speed, among many other things. The right brain is a place of creativity, peacefulness and joy. Taylor talks about having to make a choice to return from the bliss or Nirvana, as she calls it, of the right brain so her left brain could become functional again.

She had choices to make – what parts of her personality did she want to re-develop and which parts would she choose to leave behind? Her work was my introduction to the plasticity of the brain. I mention this because it gives me hope that we do have control over our thoughts. She is aware of the loops her brain makes and she says:

"When my brain runs loops that feel harshly judgmental, counterproductive or out of control I wait ninety seconds for the emotional/physiological response to dissipate and then I speak to my brain as though it is a group of children. I say, 'I appreciate your ability to think these thoughts and feel emotions, but I am really not interested in thinking these thoughts or feeling these emotions anymore. Please stop bringing this stuff up.' Essentially I am consciously asking my brain to stop hooking into specific thought patterns."[17]

As soon as I read this the first time, I began to practice it. I found that it works. But the challenge, as with all new behavior, is to remember to practice. It takes time to create any new habit and practice is the key. At night when I begin to think worrisome thoughts, I just tell my brain I am not interested and redirect my thoughts to include the most beautiful things I can think of – sometimes I concentrate on our gardens, sometimes I think about a beautiful new baby, my awesome family, something funny my grandchildren have done, the deep love my husband shows or a friend's kindness.

Wallowing in unhappiness is something I allow myself for 90 seconds or so. If it goes on longer than that, someone in my family usually reminds me I am the optimist! I'd better get on with it. That doesn't mean I don't have bad days or weeks. I do. But I try to be aware when that happens and consider what lesson I am supposed to learn from the current challenging experience. Remember, we are in control of our attitudes; and, add to that, an understanding of the control we have over our thoughts. Those thoughts include our reactions to both good experiences and painful ones.

Sometimes the brain can trick us into thinking we must or must not do something for our own safety. That is the ego talking. The ego has its place. It has been gathering information from our life since the day we were born. It thinks it is the smartest thing in the room and expects us to pay attention to whatever it tells us. The problem is that it is very good at telling us to be fearful. It isn't very highly evolved, so it may tell us to be afraid to speak in public, because when we were in first grade someone laughed at us and hurt our feelings. Our ego thinks it's not safe to speak to a group of people. Or it may tell you that you will never be a decent cook, because you failed a cooking class once. You see, it isn't all that smart because it doesn't factor in all the wonderful things we know about ourselves. It just wants to protect us, even when we don't need to be protected. Our ego subscribes to the notion that we can't be too careful. This doesn't encourage us to seek transforming opportunities

Don't get me wrong. Your ego has its place and is very necessary. However, when your rational mind and your spirit can work together you are capable of so much more than your ego might imagine. So when your ego begins the "monkey talk" in your mind, take a deep breath, hold it for a moment, and breathe out slowly. On your next breath ask your ego, "Really?" And allow your Wisdom to respond. You might sense Wisdom saying, "No, not really." And you can move on. On the other hand, Wisdom may warn you as well that it is time to listen to caution.

I'd like you to take a moment right now and think about anything new you might have read in this chapter. Take a sheet of paper and write down one or two things you've

never thought of before. Is there anything on the list that you might like to learn more about? Perhaps you'd like to read *My Stroke of Insight,* or visit Adam King's website or listen to *www.Hayhouseradio.com* for your soul. There are thousands of wonderful spiritual entrepreneurs who are ready to help you connect with your spirit/wisdom. Refer to the Resource List at the back of the book.

You might consider something you have done all your life, but maybe it doesn't fit anymore. For me, that was the way in which I practiced my faith in worship. Although I no longer belong to a Christian church, I haven't given up my faith in Spirit. My faith has shifted and grown. I feel naming myself as a Unitarian Universalist better fits who I have become. For you, maybe the way you have always eaten, or exercised doesn't fit anymore and you might consider becoming a vegetarian or vegan, a walker, runner or cyclist. It could be the way you choose your friends or activities. Maybe your social life has always been about going to a bar with your friends, but that is feeling old or outdated for you and you might try volunteering to give back to your community. Or it could be the other way around!

In other words, take a good look at how you spend your time or what absorbs your thoughts and ask if there is something you could do to kick it up a notch – is there some action that would enhance your life?

As a Spirit having a human experience, you have those five delicious senses to enjoy, play with, share and love. We were given the opportunity to be human, with hands and legs and eyes and ears and emotions and more than 90,000 miles of sensory pathways in our bodies. I believe we were made to have fun and enjoy our lives. So let's go!

In the next chapter I would like to introduce you to your Spirit. Remember that when I speak of Spirit, I mean the essence of who you are, not your personality, not what you have learned, not strengths nor weaknesses. My belief is that at your core, your essence, you are love. But let's see where Spirit takes us.

Chapter 13

Spirit

We come from love. We live in love. We return to love. I can already hear you saying, "I don't live in love! If I lived in love I wouldn't need to be reading this book." I completely understand. Most of us don't live in love every minute of every day. We have glimpses of love. We respond to love. We may give and receive love. However, I believe we can live in love. By that I mean we can be intentional (remember setting intention from Chapter 6) about living in love.

When I suggested to a friend we come from love, she told me she didn't come from love. Her mother had tried to kill her more than once when she was a child. I assured her I didn't mean her family of origin was loving. Her spirit came from love. Love is amorphous, without form. Our spirits need our bodies to have this human experience. This understanding is what makes it possible for us to separate our life experience as a physical being from our spiritual experience and our mind from both our physical being and our spiritual essence.

It doesn't matter what work you do, where you live, how much money you have, who your parents were. If you set your intention to be love, you will experience your life in a completely different way from someone who just sees their life as simply a human experience. When you feel angry, with practice, you can change that brain loop of anger. In the last chapter, you learned about the importance of practicing new behaviors and thought patterns. This is simply a continuation of that idea. You can choose to live in love.

I felt deep pain, powerlessness and fear when I was unable to overcome Bob's decision to leave our marriage. I felt betrayed, unappreciated and misunderstood when my client relationship began to crumble. I have felt unloved, invisible, ridiculed, stupid and unworthy. I have also felt powerful, disdainful, angry, loving, vengeful and fulfilled. The list can go on and on. Have you ever felt any of these things?

Because we are human, we have access to all sorts of thoughts and feelings. Our brains allow us to change our minds – literally. Some days we are filled with compassion, other days we can be filled with fury. With enlightenment we learn that in every moment we can decide what we will feel. We choose our feelings; no one gives them to us or makes them for us. It takes practice, and a good bit of it, to remember we have that much power in our lives. The reality is, we do.

Have you ever seen someone you know go through something truly horrible? Something so sad you can't imagine being able to live through it? Somehow they do. You may even see them move painfully, but gracefully through the experience. I believe we each have the power within ourselves to do that. The trick is we have to learn to ask for help from within. We must access our own Wisdom. After reading the previous chapters, I hope you are beginning to understand it is as simple as breathing into your own Wisdom.

We have an endless font of Wisdom available to us. It comes with us when we are born; we don't have to leave behind that source of love from which we come. Instead, we come in an infant body with our soul or spirit filled with Wisdom. Our challenge is that we forget what we came with. Because our culture doesn't see our soul as separate from our body, or because we value intellectual and physical ability over spiritual understanding, our spirits take a back seat in our lives. Like any other ability we might bring into this life, if it is not encouraged, called on, exercised, it will wither. I wonder what would happen to the human race if we were all taught from birth that we can always seek wisdom from within, instead of being taught that power is outside of us.

If winning wasn't what we sought, but loving was the primary aim of life, or if we weren't taught to notice differences in color or shape of skin – which are primary methods used to discriminate between people – what would our human experience be? Imagine how much easier it would be to live in love.

I remember the great anticipation I felt when my daughter and son-in-law told us they were going to have our first grandchild. I was, as a good friend likes to say, "Beyond the moon!" with excitement. I loved that little boy well before he took his first breath. I was lucky to be able to see him shortly after his arrival into this world, before he was cleaned up. There was a lovely moment, after his mother and father came out of surgery (he was a surprise C-section) and we spent time with the new mom and dad and baby, when I was able to stand by his bassinet and look into his eyes. He looked directly at my face and I was able to whisper to him, "I know you know everything. I know you will forget it all, but you do know everything you need to know." It was as if he was teaching me, showing me that his Spirit was whole. This is one of those moments in life I would never trade! That was 14 years ago. I had so much to learn, but I had intuitively begun my Spiritual journey. I was lucky enough to be able to have the same experience when his sister arrived. As Spirit would have it, she is my granddaughter and my little soul sister.

There are many spiritual entrepreneurs who encourage us to connect with Spirit. It took me years of trying to understand exactly what that meant. Along the way I thought I understood. But then I would learn something else, experience another "aha" moment and I would "know" more. I didn't expect to hear a voice or see a figure. I'm not sure what or where I thought my spirit was. As I adopted meditation as a method to dig deeply into myself, I began to realize I had been connected to Spirit all my life. Simply by breathing and focusing on a particular question or concern I began to realize my Spirit was always ready to provide Wisdom well beyond my understanding.

Remember that little girl in the hammock in Chapter 6? She was very connected to Spirit. But as the years passed and culture worked its magic, I was pretty much like every child who is immersed in her culture, except I was always curious about what I couldn't see, what might be beyond my understanding. When I was 12 years old, I bought a book about yoga. I went down to the basement in our Michigan home and lit a candle. I read the book and tried a few poses. The meditation thing was a bit beyond me, but I think I was attempting to connect to some thing or experience that would tell me more.

Maybe you have had experiences like that or quite possibly the thought of spirit has never entered your mind. Maybe you have no idea what I am even writing about here. So let me offer an example. It is something I have used for years to help people understand that we never really lose our connection to Spirit. Maybe you have seen coincidences that got you thinking that something beyond yourself was influencing your life in a positive way.

Earlier I mentioned I had developed a habit of always asking for the right words to deliver a message. I thought I was asking God or Spirit or some source outside of myself. I might have been preparing for a presentation or writing a training curriculum or a video script. I would simply stop and ask for the right words. Other times, I hadn't asked for any help. I had carefully prepared my words, but suddenly, as I was speaking, I wasn't speaking from my brain or prepared words. I was speaking from what I call "my heart." Substitute the word "heart" with "Spirit" and it becomes clear to me that I had never lost my connection.

Anyone who knows me, knows I am rarely at a loss for words. I have often felt my words were my greatest strength, because I could use them to help others. It is through my words that I feel closest to Spirit. One of my favorite understandings of God was God is a spirit. A spirit has no hands, feet, eyes or words to make something happen. So we are God's feet, hands, eyes and words. Later that belief moved to the greater understanding that we are all deeply, inextricably connected.

All life is connected and we all come from the same source, and we all share that source. That is the source I call Spirit.

I believe the source from which our spirits come is Love. Others have given it a name or created a deity. That works, too. We are only looking for ways to explain how our human experience feels, "knowing" there is something greater than our individual selves. Over many years I have moved to an understanding that we are all One. Because I believe we are all connected, I think of humanity as one living organism. I am a part of everyone and everyone is a part of me. I have been told this is very "Zen." Whatever it is, it reminds me that when I am angry with someone else, I am angry with a part of myself.

I am reminded of Buddha's quote: "Holding on to anger is like grasping a hot coal with the intent of throwing it at someone else; you are the one who gets burned."

Likewise, when we love others we are expressing something we are able to feel about ourselves. I like to think of it as our love spilling all over us. We just can't keep it contained. Once we truly experience love, we are compelled to share it.

So my Spiritual Journey has not come to an end. This part of the journey will end when I take that last breath. The practice of a Spiritual Journey is to live life. I am so happy, as a Spirit, to have the opportunity to live a human existence. I love to taste and smell, see and hear and most especially, to touch. I love the sensuousness of touch, the joy of a hug, the sweetness of kissing a baby on that soft, tiny head. Aching muscles feel like a reward for hard garden work, as does the sight of a flowering bud. You see, I love being a physical being.

My selfish and important work comes from the work I do when connected to Wisdom. I believe it is then I learn the lessons I have chosen to learn in this life. Remember it took me about 65 years to begin to actually learn my real life lessons. Deciphering the true meaning of a lifetime of learning brings joy and power.

What do I mean by power? If you choose to live your life in love, your personal power can come directly from Spirit/ Wisdom. A quick review of the chapters in this book will illustrate the kind of power you have access to every minute of every day you embrace your human experience. Let's briefly review your power sources:

1. *Implement the three simple steps (found in Chapter 1) to create change when and where you want it in your life.*
2. *You have complete control over your attitude and attitude is everything.*
3. *We are all spirits having a human experience.*

4. *Reframing often brings our life lessons into focus.*
5. *Be careful what you wish for – you might just get it.*
6. *Act with intention.*
7. *Use your breath to connect to Spirit.*
8. *Wisdom is only a breath away.*
9. *Perspective comes from living through your moments.*
10. *Create your own reality by carefully choosing the roles you will play and casting others in the role that will lead to everyone's best good.*
11. *Create and record your life intentions – make lists.*
12. *Remember that Breathing into Wisdom is a life-long practice.*
13. *Spirit and Wisdom will provide everything you need in this life – remember to ask.*

And your most powerful tool to live your best life is always remember to:
Breathe Into Wisdom
It's There, It's Yours, Use It!

Conclusion

This is my story, my life, my journey. My intention in writing this book was to share what I have learned so far in the hope that it might help you, my reader, embrace your power to live your best life, create your own reality and breathe into your own wisdom. I expect to continue to learn to tap into my Spirit and Wisdom. My hope is that you will mull over what you have read here and think about your own story, your life and your journey.

As spirits having human experiences, I believe we have two choices when it comes to living; we can let life happen to us, or we can embrace life with intention, love and action. Which choice will you make?

I encourage you to make your choice and then go for the gusto and Breathe into your own Wisdom. It's there, it's yours, use it!

If you would like to continue to learn more and acquire the workbook for *Breathe Into Wisdom*, go to *www.skrcoaching.com* and click on the Breath Into Wisdom tab. Once there, you may subscribe to my blog, "like" the "Breathe Into Wisdom" Facebook page, join the Breathe Into Wisdom online community and purchase and download your Breathe Into Wisdom workbook, mp3s and YouTube video.

You will also find information about your opportunity to work with me one-on-one as your Life Coach or participate in a Breathe Into Wisdom retreat. The schedule will be posted and updated on the website. If you are interested in having me speak at an event you may contact me through the website.

And please, Dear Soul, always remember to Breathe! Namaste.

Endnotes

[1] Bruner, Pamela, and Jack Canfield. *Tapping Into Ultimate Success.* Hay House Inc, 2012. Print.

[2] *The Tapping Solution.* Dir. Nick Ortner. Perf. Jack Canfield, Joe Vitale, Carol Look, Carol Tuttle. The Tapping Solution, LLC, 2009. DVD.

[3] Adams, Linda. "Learning a New Skill Is Easier Said Than Done." Gordon Training International. Gordon Training International. Web. 27 Sept. 2015. <http://www.gordontraining.com/free-workplace-articles/learning-a-new-skill-is-easier-said-than-done/>.

[4] Feiler, Bruce. *Abraham: A Journey to the Heart of Three Faiths.* HarperCollins Pty, 2002. Print.

[5] Idliby, Ranya, Suzanne Oliver, and Priscilla Warner. *The Faith Club: A Muslim, a Christian, a Jew--Three Women Search for Understanding.* Atria Books, 2007. Print.

[6] Nafsi, Azar. *Reading Lolita in Tehran: A Memoir in Books.* Random House Trade Paperbacks, 2008. Print.

[7] Hosseini, Khaled. *The Kite Runner.* Riverhead, 2003. Print.

[8] Mortenson, Greg. *Three Cups of Tea.* Penguin, 2008. Print.

[9] Mortenson, Greg. *Stones into Schools: Promoting Peace with Books, Not Bombs, in Afghanistan and Pakistan.* Viking Adult, 2009. Print.

[10] Diamont, Anita. *The Red Tent.* St. Martins, 1998. Print.

[11] Brooks, Geraldine. *Nine Parts of Desire: The Hidden World of Islamic Women.* Anchor, 1995. Print.

[12] Eden, Donna, and David Feinstein. *Energy Medicine.* Jeremy P. Tarcher, 1999. Print.

[13] Schucman, Helen. *A Course in Miracles-Original Edition.* Course in Miracles Society, 2009. Print.

[14] Bolte Taylor, Jill. *My Stroke of Insight: A Brain Scientist's Personal Journey.* Plume, 2009. 145-146. Print.

[15] Ibid., page 146.

[16] Webster's New World Dictionary. Third College ed. NY: Simon and Schuster, 1994. 434. Print.

[17] Taylor, page 159-160.

Resource List

The Internet offers amazing opportunities to learn from, connect to and interact with authentic, transformational practitioners without having to travel the globe. Although I have traveled across the country to meet and connect with some of the following practitioners I have more often enjoyed the benefit of their knowledge and experience through their books, online programs, DVD classes and real-time webinars.

By clicking on the link to my website you will find links to all of the spiritual entrepreneurs listed below. They are the people who have influenced my own transformation.

I'd like to introduce you to:

Christine Kloser – my mentor and one of the most beautiful souls I have ever met. This book is a direct result of her Get Your Book Done Program which is an amazing way to "birth" your own book if you believe you are called to write a transformational book. Christine "The Transformation Catalyst" powerfully combines spiritual guidance and intuition with nuts-and-bolts writing, publishing and marketing expertise – and the result is a global movement of authors who unleash their authentic voice, share their message on the pages of a book and make a difference in the world.

Donna Eden & David Feinstein – Donna and David are THE Energy Couple. Donna saved her own life by learning about her body's energy and ability to heal itself. She has spent decades teaching others. David Feinstein, Ph.D., a clinical psychologist, has served on the faculties of The Johns Hopkins University School of Medicine, Antioch College, and the California School of Professional Psychology. Donna wrote *Energy Medicine* and David wrote *Energy Psychology*. Together they recently wrote *Energies of Love*.

Nick Ortner and Jessica Ortner – a brother and sister team who worked together to create *The Tapping Solution* a documentary detailing the benefits of Emotional Freedom Tapping or EFT. Nick is the author of the book *The Tapping Solution* and *The Tapping Solution for Pain Relief*. Jessica wrote *The Tapping Solution for Weight Loss and Body Confidence*. Their work is very accessible and easy to learn. Nick's mission is to bring simple, effective, natural healing into the mainstream through Emotional Freedom Techniques (EFT) or "tapping." Tapping is a healing modality that combines ancient Chinese acupressure and modern psychology.

Pamela Bruner co-authored the book and DVD program *Tapping Into Ultimate Success* with Jack Canfield, co-creator of *Chicken Soup for the Soul*. Pamela is a Business Success Coach and the CEO of Make Your Success Real, a company designed to support transformational entrepreneurs: people whose work transforms lives and the world, including coaches, healers and consultants. Her clients build successful businesses with the help of solid business strategy and cutting-edge mindset work.

Adam King – a visionary and leader in transformational personal development. He is the creator of The Tessera Method, as well as many other programs, and experiential works. Tessera is a non-physical application that produces a neuro-physiological leverage that can result in a massive state of transformation. This is done through the use of specialized scenarios, stories and plots, sound effects, atmospheric soundscapes and powerful music.

If you would like to learn more about these spiritual entrepreneurs and others visit my website at *skrcoaching.com* where you can access information about their modalities, products and messages. I will never recommend someone whose work I am not familiar with.

About the Author

Susan K. Rothfuss has spent her life loving, learning, working and having fun. Her most fulfilling work always involves people. Her first job, while still in high school, was taking pictures of children visiting Santa Claus. After completing her B.S. in Recreation and Youth Leadership at Michigan State University, she worked with the Ingham County 4-H and the Michigan Capitol Girl Scout Council. After earning her M.B.A. from Michigan State she joined Chrysler Corporation for five years as a trainer, speech writer and marketing department program development manager. She then co-founded The  Marketing Department, Inc. (dba) TMD Consulting. For the next 20 years training, marketing and project development were her areas of concentration along with managing the local Chamber of Commerce. With each of her paid jobs she spent a good deal of her time helping people learn how to wisely answer their own questions and live their best lives. Susan is now Head Coach at SKR Coaching where invites beautiful souls to create their own pathways to fulfillment by breathing into their own wisdom in one-on-one and group sessions through speaking engagements and in retreat settings, She lives in Holt, MI with her husband Michael and close to her daughter Amy, son-in-law Tom and grandchildren Colin and Samantha.

This is her first book. You are welcome to contact her through *www.skrcoaching.com.*

Made in the USA
Middletown, DE
29 September 2016